A Pledge of the Truth

A Pledge of the Truth

Theophilus of Antioch's Doctrine of Scripture and Its Role in His *Ad Autolycum*

TAYLOR EVAN WALLS

Foreword by Michael A. G. Haykin

WIPF & STOCK · Eugene, Oregon

A PLEDGE OF THE TRUTH
Theophilus of Antioch's Doctrine of Scripture and Its Role in His *Ad Autolycum*

Copyright © 2024 Taylor Evan Walls. All rights reserved. Except for brief quotations in critical publications or reviews, no part of this book may be reproduced in any manner without prior written permission from the publisher. Write: Permissions, Wipf and Stock Publishers, 199 W. 8th Ave., Suite 3, Eugene, OR 97401.

Wipf & Stock
An Imprint of Wipf and Stock Publishers
199 W. 8th Ave., Suite 3
Eugene, OR 97401

www.wipfandstock.com

PAPERBACK ISBN: 979-8-3852-0887-6
HARDCOVER ISBN: 979-8-3852-0888-3
EBOOK ISBN: 979-8-3852-0889-0

04/05/24

Scripture quotations are from the ESV® Bible (The Holy Bible, English Standard Version®), © 2001 by Crossway, a publishing ministry of Good News Publishers. Used by permission. All rights reserved. The ESV text may not be quoted in any publication made available to the public by a Creative Commons license. The ESV may not be translated in whole or in part into any other language.

The portrait of Theophilus of Antioch is from artist Michael Burghers and included in the book: William Cave, *Apostolici: or, The history of the lives, acts, death, and martyrdoms of those who were contemporary with, or immediately succeeded the apostles: As also the most eminent of the primitive fathers of the first three hundred years. To which is added, a chronology of the three first ages of the church*. London: Printed by A.C. for Richard Chiswel, 1677. Digitized by the Pitts Digital Library and is part of the public domain. Accessed online December 19, 2023. https://dia.pitts.emory.edu/image_details.cfm?ID=5318&fbclid=IwAR1ejxBAjh3Lk-gvCQPbJFES3BK32ysV9C-WTED2Udlz7J9h3e-EeKGSsoeE

Dedicated to
Jose Jimenez, Dennis Valle, and
Oscar Bolaños,
students from 2020–2022 in the
Escuela Pastoral of Santo Domingo, Ecuador.

Contents

Foreword by Michael A. G. Haykin | ix

Preface | xi

Abbreviations | xv

Introduction | xvii

PART 1 | THEOPHILUS' WORLD, LIFE, AND THOUGHT

1 Theophilus' World and Life | 3

2 Theophilus in Recent Research | 18

3 Theophilus' Apologetic for the Christian Worldview | 26

PART 2 | THEOPHILUS' DOCTRINE OF SCRIPTURE

4 Theophilus' Bible | 51

5 "The Light of the Sun": Theophilus' Doctrine of the Necessity of Revelation | 60

6 "Counsellor and Pledge": Theophilus' Doctrine of the Authority of Scripture | 70

7 "Through One and the Same Spirit": Theophilus' Doctrine of the Inspiration of Scripture | 83

8 "More Ancient and More Trustworthy": Theophilus' Doctrine of the Antiquity and Consistency of Scripture | 94

9 Theophilus' Use of Non-Canonical Writings | 107

Contents

Conclusion | 127

Appendix 1: Theophilus' Use of Scripture | 129

Appendix 2: Outline of *Ad Autolycum* | 137

Bibliography | 141

Foreword

THEOPHILUS OF ANTIOCH (FL. c.180), who was among the first Christians to utilize the genre of apologetics to defend the Christian Faith, is by no means a household name even among those knowledgeable about the history of Christianity. His ministry was based in Antioch on the Orontes, the third largest city in the Roman Empire and a major center for Christian mission. It was the church in this city that supported Paul's missionary journeys in the Eastern Mediterranean, for example. According to Eusebius of Caesarea and Jerome, Theophilus authored a number of works, including books against two heretical teachers, Marcion, often labelled a Gnostic, and Hermogenes, who appears to have taught that God created the universe out of pre-existent matter, not *ex nihilo*. There is also mention of some catechetical works, but neither they nor the responses to Marcionism and Hermogenes have survived. The only extant work of Theophilus is his three-volume apologetic defense that was addressed to a certain Autolycus, who appears to have been a pagan friend of Theophilus.

To Autolycus contains the earliest recorded use of the Greek term *Trias*—i.e., Trinity—for the Godhead.[1] Theophilus has often been credited with the creation of this Greek term, though from the way that he employs it, the term may well have existed before him. This work also contains a mini-conversion narrative in which Theophilus relates how he came to know the One whom he calls "the living true and God."[2] One thing that is especially interesting about this narrative is the key role that Scripture played in his

---

1. Grant, *Theophilus of Antioch*, II.15.
2. Grant, *Theophilus of Antioch*, I.11.

conversion.³ Given the importance of the Scriptures in Theophilus' conversion and then in his apologetics, I am delighted that Taylor Walls has undertaken this study of the Antiochene's use of and perspective on the Bible. Here we see a snapshot of the way that Christianity, from its very beginning, was marked out as a Word-centered faith and its adherents as a "people of the Book." This is an important study of a second-century Christian author who has been greatly, and one might say, sadly, forgotten.

Dr. Michael A. G. Haykin
Dundas, Ontario
October 27, 2023.

---

3. See Grant, *Theophilus of Antioch*, I.14.

Preface

THIS BOOK FIRST BEGAN as a study in the doctrine of Scripture in the early church. At first the scope was broad and focused on all of the fathers of the second century. Though I was studying many of the other fathers as well, when I read Theophilus for the first time I was struck by his use of Scripture and the overall apologetic structure of his book. I had read many others like Clement of Alexandria and Justin Martyr who seemed too quickly to give credence to Greek philosophy and even incorporated certain Platonic ideas into their defense of Christianity. However, upon reading Theophilus, I was struck by his commitment to Scripture and the Christian worldview. Being a Reformed Presuppositionalist, I quickly saw many similarities between his apologetic and the method that I myself have sought to adopt.

My experience with Theophilus then led me to study more thoroughly his writing and apologetic method, and in 2019 I had the opportunity to present the bulk of chapter 3 of this book as a lecture for a course on Apologetics in the seminary where I then served as the Director of International Studies—Grace Bible Theological Seminary of Conway, AR. Later, I was able to incorporate other parts of this book into lectures delivered on the history of hermeneutics and the early church in the Escuela Pastoral, a church-based, pastoral training program where I serve as a full-time professor in Santo Domingo, Ecuador.

It then transitioned into the content of the thesis for my Master of Divinity with Reformed Baptist Seminary. I am very grateful for the help of my advisor, Dr. Michael Haykin, who helped me to narrow my overly broad scope to focus on Theophilus, and who also made other helpful suggestions for research and style. His guidance has also been key in turning the thesis into a manuscript and helping to have it published. I am very grateful for his help, guidance, and desire to see this work in print, and am also forever grateful for his recommendation of this work and for contributing the foreword. This work would definitely not be what you have before you without his help. However, any weaknesses in it are all mine.

Due to the thesis phase of this work, I have sought to write to a broader audience and in a more academic context. However, I was constantly thinking about my pastoral students who desire to serve Christ's church in pastoral ministry and how a better understanding of the Scriptures in the early church and the writing of Theophilus specifically could help them in their service to Christ's church. I hope that this book will help them and others like them who love studying the Bible and church history to appreciate the riches of our heritage in the early church. Also, I hope that they will follow Theophilus' example and always seek to be faithful to Scripture, in faith, practice, and apologetic, even though it may cost them greatly. Just as Theophilus was possibly risking his life as he wrote his apology, I hope they too will wear the name "Christian" proudly though it may mean ostracization, persecution, or death. For this reason, I have dedicated this book to them.

I want to take the opportunity to thank several individuals who have been instrumental in my life and ministry and in the production of this book. I want to thank Dr. Jeffrey Johnson and Danny Thursby, my pastors, colaborers, and friends, who have been very helpful in forming my theology, my apologetic, and always being there to listen when I needed to talk over all the different arguments and points as I was studying this material. Likewise, I am thankful to my friend and colaborer on the field in Ecuador, Jorge Rodriguez, who is a constant source of sound advice and pastoral encouragement.

I am also thankful for my friend Dr. Robert Gonzales, who was the secondary reader for my thesis, and who offered helpful tips for formatting and style, and has also encouraged me to see this book published. Likewise, I am thankful for Ron Miller who looked over my manuscript and pointed out several typos. He also has been very helpful in forming my understanding of the history of the church.

I am also thankful to Dr. Stuart Parsons who not only has helped me through his various writings on Theophilus which are cited repeatedly in this book, but also for providing helpful comments on the pre-publication manuscript of this book and being willing to provide his endorsement. I

Preface

see this book as building on the very firm foundation that he has laid in his doctoral dissertation and his book, *Ancient Apologetic Exegesis*. His treatment on the rhetorical use of Scripture in Theophilus has been essential for my understanding of Theophilus' structure and doctrine of Scripture.

Finally, I am thankful to the Lord for giving us his Word and raising up godly men in church history and in our own day. He has brought key men into my life, both living and deceased, who have been formative in my thinking and understanding of Scripture. I am thankful for him opening my eyes and removing the scales so that I might see the glorious truth of the Gospel and love his Word. I am also thankful for him converting Theophilus and using and preserving his work for us to learn from today. This book flows from a commitment to his Lordship in all areas of life and study, and I pray that I have been faithful to him in the various stages of this work. I write this book "in the hope of being useful to God,"[1] and my utmost prayer is that he would be glorified in it and in the lives of those who read its pages. *Soli Deo Gloria!*

Taylor Evan Walls
Santo Domingo, Ecuador
December 17, 2023

---

1. Grant, *Theophilus of Antioch*, I.1

Abbreviations

AA	Theophilus, *Ad Autolycum*
ANF	Alexander Roberts and James Donaldson, eds. *Ante-Nicene Fathers*. Buffalo, NY: Christian Literature Company.
NPNF	Philip Schaff, *Nicene and Post-Nicene Fathers*. Buffalo, NY: Chritian Literature Company.

S. THEOPHILUS ANTIOCHENUS.

Introduction

If you will, read these books carefully so that you may have a counsellor and pledge of the truth. (AA III.30)

IN HIS CLASSIC WORK on the spirituality of the early church, Robert Louis Wilken has famously said,

> But what has impressed me most is the omnipresence of the Bible in early Christian writings. Early Christian thought is biblical, and one of the lasting accomplishments of the patristic period was to forge a way of thinking, scriptural in language and inspiration, that gave to the church and to Western civilization a unified and coherent interpretation of the Bible as a whole.[1]

What Wilken says generally of the early church, can also be said particularly of the only remaining writing of Theophilus of Antioch, his three books *Ad Autolycum*, in which the Bible is likewise "omnipresent."

Theophilus is one of the oft-forgotten fathers of the second century who, among other things, sought to defend the Christian faith from those who opposed it. Many Greeks and Romans of the second century held in great esteem the philosophical and religious customs of the Roman empire and saw Christianity as a major threat to their way of life. For this reason, Theophilus sets out to use Scripture, making use of many of the

---

1. Wilken, *The Spirit of Early Christian Thought,* loc. 57.

Introduction

Old Testament books as well as several New Testament books, to show the superiority of the Christian faith and its divine authority and complete consistency over all the writings and claims of the Greek poets, philosophers, and historians.

This book seeks to respond to modern critiques of conservative approaches to the Bible and their claims of continuity with the second century. Most notably, Craig Allert has affirmed that many scholars do not provide thorough analyses of the scriptural thought of the early church fathers, and that their use is selective and does not appreciate the role of non-canonical works.[2] Allert identifies a significant issue in how many studies of the early church and the canon make brushstroke affirmations that are based on certain truths, but tend to minimize difficulties (like the use of non-canonical works), read in one's own understanding of certain terms (like "inspiration"), and often do not include an in-depth study of individual fathers. Though the books that came to be part of our Bible undoubtedly played an important role in the early church fathers, yet how each father understood the nature and inspiration of Scripture and Scripture's relationship with non-canonical works has not been sufficiently considered. Therefore, this book hopes to revive an appreciation for Theophilus in particular, who sadly has been overlooked in many studies of the early church or the development of the canon, and to blaze a trail for others to take up the task of giving thorough presentations of the way individual church fathers understood the nature of the Bible's authority and inspiration.

Scripture plays a foundational role in Theophilus' defense of Christianity as he presents the Christian Scriptures as the only consistent and divinely-inspired source of truth and ethics. In fact, Scripture appears to play such a role in his thought because of the role it played in his own conversion. As he says, "At that time I encountered the sacred writings of the holy prophets, who through the Spirit of God foretold past events in the way that they happened, present events in the way they are happening, and future events in the order in which they will be accomplished."[3] Therefore, he develops a defense of Scripture that is openly committed to the authority and faithfulness of Scripture. He uses Scripture by making several lengthy and strategically-placed citations, weavings webs of scriptural allusions that rhetorically undergird his arguments, and even imitating scriptural patterns and structures. Through this "omnipresent" use of Scripture in his work,

2. Allert, *A High View of Scripture?*.
3. Grant, *Theophilus of Antioch*, I.14.

INTRODUCTION

Theophilus gives us a clear glimpse into his understanding of the nature of Scripture. At one point, he calls for his reader to search the Scriptures and there find a sure "counsellor" and a "pledge of the truth": "If you will, read these books carefully so that you may have a counsellor and pledge of the truth."[4] In other words, for Theophilus, the only sure way to get to the truth about God, the world—past, present, or future—, man, or ethics is not found in the Greek philosophers but rather in the diligent study of the Scriptures of the Law, the Prophets, the Gospels, and the Apostles.

Therefore, this book seeks to give a thorough presentation of what Theophilus thought and believed about Scripture, at least as far as can be determined from his only extant work. It seeks to provide a deeper understanding of what he affirmed concerning the necessity, authority, inspiration, antiquity, and consistency of Scripture in light of his second-century context and of the overall argument structure of his apology. Also, this book seeks to give a balanced presentation of his view of inspiration by analyzing the phenomena of the appearance of non-canonical works in his argument.

A secondary purpose of this book is to foster a greater appreciation for the early church in the lives and studies of modern Christians. Many evangelicals today hear references to the church fathers and their alarms go off and they think that the person might be a Roman Catholic or Eastern Orthodox. Many modern Christians have cut themselves off from a great wealth of theology, exegesis, and spirituality that is not without its consequences. Due to the importance of Scripture for evangelicals, many have avoided the early church for fear of it becoming an authoritative tradition over the Scriptures. For this reason, this book hopes to show the modern Christian that he has more in common with Christians in the second century than he might realize. This book not only hopes to foster appreciation and deeper study of Theophilus specifically, but also the other church fathers of the second century and beyond.[5]

This book consists of two main parts. The first three chapters give an introduction to Theophilus: his life, his work, his world, and his thought. These chapters help to put Theophilus in his context to aid in a better understanding of his thinking and argumentation. Chapter 1 looks at the world of the second-century church and introduces some of the other writings in this period as well as some of the cultural trends that are seen in the

---

4. Grant, *Theophilus of Antioch*, III.30.

5. For a more thorough attempt at achieving this goal, see Haykin, *Rediscovering the Church Fathers*.

background of Theophilus' writing. It then introduces the life of Theophilus and gives an introduction to the purpose, style, and later influence of his work *Ad Autolycum*. Chapter 2 looks at Theophilus from the modern perspective and summarizes some of the major trends in modern scholarship on Theophilus from the last 150 years or so. This chapter summarizes three major areas of discussion: his view of Christ, the Trinity, and Scripture. Chapter 3 then looks more closely at Theophilus' work and seeks to summarize his worldview system as presented in *Ad Autolycum*. This chapter shows how his work narrates the clash of two worldviews—the Christian or biblical worldview and the pagan worldview. There are three major battlegrounds where this war takes place: in the realm of ontology, ethics, and epistemology. His thought on each of these points is summarized, and its importance for his apologetic argument is considered.

The second major part represents the heart of this book and consists in chapters 4–9. Chapter 4 looks at the nature of the Bible in Theophilus' time and what can be gleaned about the contents of his canon from his work. It also summarizes the ways in which Theophilus makes use of Scripture. Chapters 5 through 8 then look at several attributes of Scripture as affirmed explicitly or implied rhetorically in Theophilus. These chapters highlight specifically his affirmations with respect to the (1) the necessity of the Scriptures (ch. 5), (2) their authority (ch. 6), (3) their inspiration (ch. 7), and (4) their antiquity and (5) consistency (ch. 8). The final chapter then looks at how the books that came to be known as canonical were not the only writings used in Theophilus' argument. This chapter analyzes the role that few allusions to apocryphal or pseudepigraphal writings of Christian or Jewish origin played in his writing as well as the significant appearance of the Greek Sibyl whom he views as a prophet sent by God among the Greeks.

PART 1

Theophilus' World, Life, and Thought

1

Theophilus' World and Life

INDIVIDUAL CHRISTIANS AND CHURCHES were seeking to work out the implications of their Christian faith for their everyday life, many were taking up the pen to defend Christianity from false accusations and seeking to obtain some leniency in public policy towards Christians, and others were having to defend the faith of the Church from attacks from Gnosticism that had developed into a full-fledged alternative to the Christian faith in Christian terms. These are some of the major issues that befell the church in the second century. Before going to the heart of this book, it is important to see Theophilus in his historical context. This chapter will first look at the world of the second century in which Theophilus lived. Then, it will look at Theophilus specifically and the unfortunately little that we know about his life. Finally, it will give an introduction to his only extant work that provides the basis for the claims made later in this book.

THE WORLD OF THEOPHILUS

The second century was an important period in church history; however, it is often overlooked due to the towering significance of the apostolic period before, and the time of Constantine and Nicaea after. In the words of Michael Kruger, the second century was when "Christianity [was] at the crossroads." He describes it more fully in this way: "This particular block of time is one of the most critical in the life of the Church—perhaps the moment when it was most vulnerable. It is what we might call the *transitional* century for the early Christian faith. The Church was out of the apostolic womb and now trying to take its first breath."[1]

With the death of the apostles and their disciples,[2] the church lost a formidable force in its fight against heresies. This loss led to a greater openness among heretics and greater diversity in groups seeking to be seen as the true Christians.[3] Even in the New Testament the seeds of major second-century groups like the Gnostics and the Ebionites can be seen.[4] Gnosticism was a highly Greek-influenced version of Christianity that generally denied the value of the physical realm and denied Christ's physical Incarnation and the physical resurrection, much like the false teachers of Colossians,[5] First Timothy,[6] and First John.[7] Marcion, who began teaching his heresy in the 140s had some similarities with the Gnostics, but he set himself apart by an explicit denial of the Old Testament Scriptures, claiming they presented a different God than the one who identifies himself as the Father of the Lord Jesus. He also had a modified New Testament canon that only included a version of Luke and the Pauline epistles.[8]

---

1. Kruger, *Christianity at the Crossroads*, 1.

2. Polycarp was one of the last known disciples of the apostle John when he was martyred in 155/6 AD.

3. Cf. Hegssipus, "Fragments of his five books of commentaries on the acts of the church," ANF 8:764.

4. It is often affirmed that the New Testament bears witness to the beginning of Gnostic thought, though we do not see a full-fledged Gnosticism until the second century. Cf. Ferguson, *Backgrounds of Early Christianity*, 301–12.

5. Cf. Moo, *The Letters to the Colossians and to Philemon*, 52–3.

6. Skarsaune, «Heresy and the Pastoral Epistles», 9–11.

7. Ferguson gives this summary of the major unifying tennets of Gnosticism, though he recognizes the difficulty of generalizing: "The most nearly common features of the sources treated under the heading of Gnosticism are a distinction between the creator(s) and controllers of the material world and the ultimate transcendent divine being, an interest in speculation about the nature of divinity and the heavenly realm, consideration of the cause of the human condition with a focus on the soul's eventual transcendence of the created order, patterns of spirituality consistent with this worldview, and the interpretation of Jewish or Christian Scripture traditions in advancing the viewpoint." Ferguson, *Backgrounds of Early Christianity*, 301.

8. Most of what we know about the Gnostics and Marcion has come from Irenaeus's work, *Against Heresies* books 1 and 2. Much of his presentation has been confirmed by the manuscript finds at Nag Hammadi. Cf. Irenaeus of Lyons, *St. Irenaeus of Lyons:*

The Ebionites, on the other hand, were a highly Jewish-influenced group who affirmed the continued necessity of observing Jewish rituals in order to be a Christian, much like the Judaizers that were the object of Paul's attack in Galatians and the whole church's censure in Acts 15. Later in the second century (ca. 171 AD) another group appeared in Phrygia, who claimed to have received special revelations of the Spirit, and their leader, Montanus, was later thought to have been the promised Paraclete of John 14–16.[9]

Not only did the second-century Christians have battles from within (speaking broadly), but they also lived in a time when it was socially and philosophically unacceptable to be a Christian. The second century was a time of great persecution and social ostracization. There is evidence of regional persecutions that led to the death of Ignatius of Antioch (ca. 107), and also in Bithynia where the proconsul Pliny the Younger had correspondence with the emperor Trajan over the proper treatment of the Christians.[10] This did not establish an empire-wide persecution, but it did give leeway for local leaders to use their judgement in order to maintain peace in ways they deemed best. There is also the famous account of the martyrdom of Polycarp that seems to have been the result of a public outcry against the Christians of Smyrna (ca. AD 155).[11] About a decade later, Justin was martyred in Rome.[12] However, the most famous persecutions in this time were the result of the more negative attitude of Marcus Aurelius (AD 161–180) toward the Christians. This led to a forceful and atrocious persecution of Christians in Gaul, especially Vienne and Lyons around 177 AD, and shortly after the emperor's death there was another round of persecutions in North Africa that is seen in the Scillitan Martyrs (ca. AD 181).[13]

Apart from the regional, political persecution that led to secrecy about Christian practices and worship, and at certain times even martyrdom, the second-century Christians were also attacked on the philosophical battleground. Due to the secrecy about their meetings to which they were forced,

---

Against the Heresies, Book 1; St. Irenaeus of Lyons, *St. Irenaeus of Lyons: Against the Heresies, Book 2*.

9. Grant, *Greek Apologists of the Second Century*, 87–9; Eusebius, *Ecclesiastical History*, 5.3.4.

10. Stevenson, *A New Eusebius*, 18–21.

11. Cf. *The Martyrdom of Polycarp*; Stevenson, *New Eusebius*, 22–30; Eusebius, *Ecclesiastical History*, 4.14–15.

12. Stevenson, *New Eusebius*, 32–34; Eusebius, *Ecclesiastical History*, 4.16.

13. Stevenson, *New Eusebius*, 34–45; ANF 9:285.

there were wild speculations about what occurred there, which gave the Christians a reputation for immorality of the grossest sorts. They were seen as enemies of the gods and thus enemies of Roman tradition and even the Roman people.[14]

It is in this context of battles with heresies and political and philosophical persecution that we find the main body of literature from the second century, the Greek Apologists.[15] Some of these men took on the task of tackling heresies, most notably Irenaeus who devoted five volumes to the topic under the title *The Detection and Overthrow of Knowledge Falsely So-Called*, but also including Theophilus (though his anti-heretical works are no longer extant). However, many of them saw the necessity of writing apologies, or defenses, for the Christian faith. Authors like Aristides of Athens, Justin Martyr, Apollinaris of Hierapolis, Melito of Sardis, and Athenagoras of Athens all wrote philosophical treatises to the emperor seeking tolerance, or at least the recognition of their right to exist. On the other hand, the anonymous *Letter to Diognetus*,[16] Tatian's *Oration to the Greeks*, and Theophilus' *Ad Autolycum* were written to individual pagans or pagan readers in general (e.g. Tatian) in hopes of delivering Christianity from the many false accusations levied against it.

It is important to see Theophilus in this context.[17] As he writes and engages in open dialogue with his pagan friend Autolycus, he was certainly

---

14. Stevenson, *New Eusebius*, 58–67. Justin Martyr and Tertullian respond to this secrecy by giving accounts of what occurred in Christian services and their agape feasts. Justin describes the church service in his *First Apology* 65–7. Tertullian describes Christian practices, and the agape feasts in particular, in his *Apology* 39.

15. For a condensed history of the church in the second century see chapters 3 and 4 of Chadwick, *The Early Church*. cf. Kruger, *Christianity at the Crossroads*. For a broader and more detailed presentation of the context of the church in the first three centuries, see Ferguson, *Early Christians Speak*. For a thorough treatment of the Greek Apologists, see Grant, *Greek Apologists of the Second Century*; Young, "Greek Apologists of the Second Century," 81–104. Other helpful resources on the second century are: Osborne, *The Emergence of Christian Theology*; Paget and Lieu, *Christianity in the Second Century*; Grant, "The Social Setting of Second-Century Christianity," 16–29.

16. For a fuller treatment of this short but interesting apology, see Haykin, *Rediscovering the Church Fathers*, 49–68.

17. Parsons has this helpful comment about Theophilus in this context: "In light of the severity and recurrence of Roman persecution, it would not have been surprising if Theophilus had adopted a bitter or fearful tone toward Roman non- Christians, or if he had refused to correspond with any of them. It is therefore surprising to find that Theophilus sent three book-length letters to Autolycus, in which he tried to persuade him to forsake worship of the Greco-Roman gods and to embrace Christianity.

opening himself up to great risk.[18] According to the policy established by Trajan, Christians were not to be hunted, but if they were found, they were to be condemned if they would not offer incense to the emperor or Roman gods. Therefore, it was a bold move for Theophilus, and the other apologists, to openly engage in this type of interaction and to profess plainly that they were Christians.[19] Certainly, Theophilus was not alone in this boldness and openness about his faith. Justin Martyr, for example, often held open classes where he would instruct people in the true philosophy of Christianity. It was actually a debate opponent, Crescens, who turned him in, leading to his martyrdom.[20] Theophilus boldly and openly expresses this commitment to Christianity in these words: ". . . [F]uthermore you call me a Christian as if I were bearing an evil name, I acknowledge that I am a Christian. I bear this name beloved by God in the hope of being useful to God. It is not the case, as you suppose, that the name of God is offensive."[21]

THE LIFE OF THEOPHILUS

Theophilus finds himself in the middle of many of the various "crossroads" that the second-century church had to face. He sought to present a faithful and convincing defense of the Christian faith against the Pagans who slandered or persecuted them. He sought to stand for scriptural truth against heresies that were wreaking havoc in the church after the death of the apostles. He also can be seen in the overall trajectory of the church in its pursuit of what became Nicene clarity on the doctrine of the Trinity. He can be placed in a common place with many other fathers of the second-century

---

Throughout these three letters, which are typically collectively entitled 'To Autolycus' or *Ad Autolycum*, Theophilus exhibited neither anger, bitterness, nor fear towards Autolycus on account of Roman persecution against Christians. While he sharply critiqued Greco-Roman religious ideas in the letters, Theophilus nevertheless maintained a friendly tone." Parsons, "By One and the Same Spirit," 2.

18. Citations of AA come from Grant, *Theophilus of Antioch*. Current reference at III.30. Citations to this work are given with respect to their placement in the book and chapter of AA and not with respect to the page number. This method is used because Grant's translation maintains the chapter divisions of AA and thus each citation can easily be found in it, but also so that the reader may see the same citation in other translations at hand.

19. Grant, *Theophilus of Antioch*, I.1, 12.

20. Stevenson, *New Eusebius*, 32–34.

21. Grant, *Theophilus of Antioch*, I.1

church with respect to his understanding of the limits of the canon. He also provides a bridge between the apologetic exegesis of his contemporaries and the more formal commentary that becomes more prominent in the third century. Theophilus was in no way alone in all of these endeavors, however, this book seeks to foster a greater appreciation for the role that the often-overlooked Theophilus might have played in the development of the early church and its use and understanding of Scripture.

As to the personal history of Theophilus, it is a sad fact of history that very little of his work and his life has been preserved for the modern reader.[22] He grew up in a pagan home but had a conversion experience when he came across the Scriptures and, being convinced of their superiority to the other philosophies he had studied, he believed the Word of God.[23] According to Eusebius, in 168 AD he was ordained as the sixth bishop of Antioch in Syria, where Ignatius (AD 30–107) had been much earlier.[24] His ministry must have continued into the reign of Commodus (AD 181–192), during which AA book 3 was written.[25]

Theophilus wrote dogmatic treatises defending orthodoxy against Marcionism and commentaries on the Gospels and the book of Proverbs.[26] However, the only remaining work of his consists of three apologetic books written to Autolycus, a pagan with whom Theophilus had had extensive personal conversation. From this work we learn that Theophilus was not only well-versed in the Scriptures, but he was also educated in Greek philosophy,[27] a fond student of history and chronology,[28] and a fan of puns.[29]

---

22. Cf. Schaff, *The History of the Church*, 732–5; Svebakken, "Theophilus of Antioch," 542–43.

23. Grant, *Theophilus of Antioch*, I.14.

24. Eusebius, *Ecclesiastical History*, 1.4.19.

25. Grant, *Greek Apologists*, 143; Grant, *Theophilus of Antioch*, III.27.

26. Jerome, *Lives of Illustrious Men*, in NPNF 2.3: ch. 25. It appears that Jerome might have doubted the validity of the commentary on the gospels that bore Theophilus' name. See Sanday, "A Commentary on the Gospels Attributed to Theophilus of Antioch," 89–101.

27. Due to some inaccuracies in Theophilus' use of some of the Greek sources, it is possible that he had direct experience and study in Homer and Hesiod but that his understanding of the Greek philosophers probably came from doxographies, or collections of quotes from philosophers organized somewhat systematically for instructional purposes; Grant, "Problem of Theophilus," 180–8.

28. Grant, *Theophilus of Antioch*, III.16–30.

29. Grant, *Theophilus of Antioch*, I.1, 12.

Eusebius and Jerome knew of his works and some of their affirmations depend on a familiarity with at least part of them. Eusebius says this about Theophilus:

> Of Theophilus, whom we have mentioned as bishop of the church of the Antiochians, three elementary [στοιχειώδη; stoicheiōdē] treatises are extant, addressed to Autolycus, and another with the title, *Against the Heresy of Hermogenes*, in which he has quoted the Apocalypse of John, and there are also extant some other books of his on instruction. Heretics were even then no less defiling the pure seed of apostolic teaching like tares, and the shepherds of the churches in every place, as though driving off wild beasts from Christ's sheep, excluded them at one time by rebukes and exhortations to the brethren, at another by their more complete exposure, by unwritten and personal inquiry and conversation, and ultimately correcting their opinions by accurate arguments in written treatises. It is clear that Theophilus joined with the others in this campaign against them from a noble treatise which he made against Marcion, which has been preserved until now with the others that we have mentioned.[30]

It is clear that Eusebius did not think of Theophilus as an almost Ebionite heretic as mentioned by Grant.[31] He was seen as among the ranks of those who were valiant for the truth and defended it against the various heresies that became popular in the second century.[32] However, in reference to AA

---

30. Eusebius, *The Ecclesiastical History*, 385 [= 4.24.1].

31. Grant, "The Problem of Theophilus," 180. Cf. Grant, *Jesus After the Gospels*, 68–82. In the second reference he says that Theophilus was closer to Theodotus, the adoptionist, than anything. However, the condemnations of Theodotus by Eusebius (*Ecclesiastical History*, 5.28.6) definitely make it strange, if this was his position expressed more fully in other works unknown to us, that Eusebius would speak of him as a defender of the faith against heresy. At the same time, it could also be due to a mere superficial familiarity with Theophilus.

32. Though of course there are references to heresies even in the New Testament: such as in Galatians 1, Colossians, 1 John, etc., the early church historian Hegesippus says that it was not until the death of the apostles and their immediate descendants that the heretics became much bolder in their fight against the truth: "Up to that period [before the death of the Apostles] the Church had remained like a virgin pure and uncorrupted: for, if there were any persons who were disposed to tamper with the wholesome rule of the preaching of salvation, they still lurked in some dark place of concealment or other. But, when the sacred band of apostles had in various ways closed their lives, and that generation of men to whom it had been vouchsafed to listen to the Godlike Wisdom with their own ears had passed away, then did the confederacy of godless error take its rise through the treachery of false teachers, who, seeing that none of the apostles any

in particular, he describes the three books as "elementary." This may seem like a jab at its contents, and has been understood in this way by some,[33] but in light of the use of the root of στοιχειώδη (*stoicheiōdē*) by Eusebius in other parts of his work, it appears to describe a work that contains propaedeutic or introductory material. A form of this same root also appears in Hebrews 5:12 (στοιχεῖα; *stoicheia*) which Theophilus alludes to in II.25. This is in accord with the argument of Parsons in which he proposes that the protreptic style of Theophilus is parallel to the affirmation of the writer of Hebrews in 5:12–6:2 where he encourages them to leave the *elementary principles* of Christianity of repentance, faith, initiation rites, resurrection, and eternal judgment.[34] In fact, apart from initiation rites,[35] these elementary principles mentioned by the author of Hebrews are some of the main points defended by Theophilus in his book. Therefore, it seems that Eusebius is seeking to highlight how Theophilus' apologetic is an introductory work to the basic principles of the Christian faith.

Moreover, Jerome is even more positive in his presentation of Theophilus. In his *Lives of Illustrious Men* 25, he affirms,

> Theophilus, sixth bishop of the church of Antioch, in the reign of the emperor Marcus Antoninus Verus composed a book *Against Marcion*, which is still extant, also three volumes *To Autolycus* and one *Against the heresy of Hermogenes* and other short and elegant treatises, well fitted for the edification of the church. I have read, under his name, commentaries *On the Gospel* and *On the proverbs of Solomon* which do not appear to me to correspond in style and language with the elegance and expressiveness of the above works.[36]

---

longer survived, at length attempted with bare and uplifted head to oppose the preaching of the truth by preaching 'knowledge falsely so called.'" Hegesippus, "Fragments from His Five Books of Commentaries on the Acts of the Church," ANF 8:764.

33. Whittaker, "Review of *Theophilus of Antioch: Ad Autolycum*," 235. Also, Grant says, "Eusebius described the books as 'elementary,' a term he also applied to the *Shepherd of Hermas* to indicate its lack of style and sophisticated theology. . . . The term seemed appropriate for Theophilus' work and, no doubt, his theology." Grant, *Greek Apologists*, 144.

34. Parsons, *Ancient Apologetic Exegesis*, ch. 2.

35. He does briefly mention baptism in his allegorical interpretation of the creation of the ocean inhabitants on the fifth day, but he does not spend more time discussing initiation rites. This would be a further argument against the proposal that AA is of a catechetical genre. Cf. Grant, *Theophilus of Antioch*, II.16.

36. Jerome, "Lives of Illustrious Men," ch. 25 in NPNF II.3.369.

Jerome refers to the three main treatises of Theophilus as "elegant" and "well fitted for the edification of the church." It is interesting to note the distinction between the "elementary" books to Autolycus mentioned by Eusebius, and the elegant and edifying works of Theophilus mentioned here. Maybe Jerome is thinking more particularly in one or both of the books that are no longer extant but known then to him. Another possibility is that Jerome saw that, in spite of his elementary and protreptic style, AA was still fit for edifying and instructing the church. However, it is also clear that Jerome did not question the orthodoxy of Theophilus as has been done by many modern scholars.[37]

These affirmations that come from 1500–1600 years closer to Theophilus' time than the modern authors who have written on Theophilus, stand in stark contrast to the way in which many have described him and his work. One reviewer referred to him as "not stimulating reading . . . so that the general effect is flaccid and trite. . . . the work is ill-organized."[38] While Bennett Pascal says,

> As early as the second century, the apologetic of Theophilus is a *crambe repetita* made up of stock polemics, as well as chronological arguments borrowed from Josephus to certify the antiquity of Biblical authority. The style is jejune, although it occasionally displays a grandeur of concept, or a little poetic lustre borrowed from the Psalmists and Prophets.[39]

Walter Bauer also said, "To me, there is no comparison between the superior theologian Irenaeus and the shallow babbler of the *Apology to Autolycus*."[40] The notable scholar of early church history, Henry Chadwick, also described this work as a "rambling defence of Christianity."[41] And, according to Robert Grant, Theophilus "was unable to understand clearly either the Christian faith or the Hellenistic philosophies opposed to it."[42] In another place, Grant says, "Theophilus's arrangement of his materials thus

---

37. Cf. Rogers, "Theophilus of Antioch," 214–5.
38. Whittaker, "Review of *Theophilus of Antioch: Ad Autolycum*," 235.
39. C. Pascal, "Review of *Theophilus of Antioch, Ad Autolycum* by Robert M. Grant," 94.
40. Bauer, *Heresy and Orthodoxy in Earliest Christianity*, 18, n. 38.
41. Chadwick, *The Early Church*, Loc. 1163; ch. 4.
42. Grant, *After the New Testament*, 150. Cited in Parsons, *Ancient Apologetic Exegesis*, ch. 1.

leaves something to be desired, and his insistently didactic tone often fails to retain the reader's attention."[43]

THEOPHILUS' AD AUTOLYCUM

Theophilus' only extant work is his three books written to a pagan friend, Autolycus. It has been proposed that Autolycus is merely a rhetorical character and that Theophilus is really writing to paganism in general. Though unlikely, this proposal does have a hint of truth. Theophilus does direct his address to his friend Autolycus in particular, but he understands that he is also writing for posterity who will read his works. In III.23 he prays and asks for God's favor "so that you [Autolycus] and everyone who reads these books may be led by his truth and grace." Therefore, though the book must be understood with respect to his immediate audience of Autolycus, he can also be seen to be writing for the benefit of others.[44] This might also be the idea behind Jerome's affirmation of his book being "well fitted for the edification of the church."[45]

Theophilus and Autolycus appear to have had several personal conversations on the nature of Christianity, but Autolycus continues to maintain his hostility. The first two books appear to be more closely knit together than they are with the third. It is possible that the first two books were written slightly before 177, since he refers to the emperor in a singular form, and it was only during 168–177 that Marcus Aurelius reigned alone. It is also possible that they came early in the reign of Commodus. However, the use of the first two books by Irenaeus in the 180s and Tertullian in the late 190s in Carthage may lend support to the idea that the first two were written earlier than the third.[46] The third book was definitely written during

---

43. Grant, *Ad Autolycum*, xi. Parsons affirms that this lack of appreciation for the structure and style of Theophilus is due to a modern (anachronistic) perspective on Theophilus' ancient rhetoric. He thus shows the importance of seeing Theophilus in the context of other sources of ancient rhetoric and how Scripture allusions and citations play a key role in that rhetoric. According to him, and as evidenced in these various quotes, if we miss this ancient rhetorical context, we miss Theophilus. Parsons, *Ancient Apologetic Exegesis*, ch. 4.

44. Cf. Parsons, "By One and the Same Spirit," 2, n. 2.

45. Jerome, "Lives of Illustrious Men," ch. 25 in NPNF II.3.369.

46. Grant affirms that there appears to be more literary dependence between Books 1 and 2, and that book 3 does not really depend on the prior books: "this book is independent of the others and does not presuppose their contents;" Grant, *Greek Apologists*, 144.

the reign of Commodus (AD 181–192) as the final date mentioned in his chronology of the world is the death of Marcus Aurelius (AD 180).[47]

Purpose

Book 1 does not have as clear of a purpose statement as do the other two, but there are two main allegations he is trying to rectify: (1) he wants to demonstrate the foolishness of the man-made idols of which Autolycus boasted, and (2) he wants to give an account of why it is not a dreadful thing to be called a Christian. In the midst of this critique of man-made idols, he also seeks to show the true way by which men can know the invisible God. This point thus provides the connection between his answer to the first and second critique, since it is only the Christian religion that provides the remedy to the problem that has blinded man's eyes so that he cannot see or know God and prefers to serve idols.

Book 2 begins with this purpose statement: "[1] to provide for you . . . a more accurate proof concerning the pointless labour and pointless worship in which you are confined. [2] I shall use a few of those histories books which you read—though perhaps you do not yet understand them—in order to make the truth plain to you."[48] This book thus focuses on two goals. First, he seeks to show the folly and inconsistency of the various Greek writings and to contrast them with the harmony and glory of the Scriptures. It is in this book that he spends the most time directly dealing with Scripture, thus providing the bulk of the argument of this book.[49]

Book 3 begins with the programmatic phrase: "though after meeting us you still regard [1] the word of truth as silly, [2] fancying that our scriptures are new and modern."[50] Here, he presents the two main accusations that he refutes in Book 3. He tackles the first by showing how the word of truth is consistent and presents the only genuine, life-changing rule for life. He handles the second accusation by giving a chronology of

---

However, this is false. He often refers to things said before in the previous dialogues, and even in III.19 says, "as we have explained in the second volume," which is a reference to the details discussed in II.30–31.

47. Grant, *Greek Apologists*, 143–144. Cf. Grant, *Theophilus of Antioch*, III.27.
48. Grant, *Theophilus of Antioch*, II.1.
49. Grant, *Theophilus of Antioch*, II.10–35.
50. Grant, *Theophilus of Antioch*, III.1

the world by which he seeks to prove the historicity of Christianity and its writings.[51]

In all three books, Theophilus seeks to present the superiority of Christianity over against the philosophies of the Greek historians, poets, and philosophers. He seeks to show the folly of idolatry, the inconsistency and immorality of Greek philosophy, and at the same time how Christianity alone can give an adequate account of God, the world, and ethics. In light of this purpose, it is fitting that more recent scholarship on Theophilus has shifted away from seeing his work as catechetical to seeing it as protreptic.[52] The protreptic style is that by which a writer seeks to demonstrate the falsehood of opposing philosophies and establish the superiority of his own.

Style and Genre

The protreptic style is important to keep in mind, and it also accounts for the important use of rhetoric in all three books.[53] The style and genre of AA can be illustrated by a courtroom scene. Autolycus is the prosecutor and Theophilus the defense attorney. They are seeking to determine the superior philosophy, paganism or Christianity. And, as Parsons points out, the material witnesses for their various arguments are their respective authoritative texts: "[textual] Witness interrogation serves as the 'meta-logic' of Theophilus' apologetic."[54] Theophilus uses Scripture to show the authority, consistency, harmony, antiquity, and the superior ethic of the Christian worldview, along with corroborating evidence from the Sibyl and the occasional statement of poet and philosopher. To critique Autolycus's worldview, he calls various literary witnesses from among the pagan literature, including Homer, Hesiod, and various philosophers from doxographical sources, to show their own inconsistency, pride, and falsehood.[55]

---

51. For a detailed outline of the three books see Appendix 2: Outline of Ad Autolycus.

52. Rogers, "Theophilus of Antioch;" Parsons, *Ancient Apologetic Exegesis*. The idea of a catechetical genre may flow from a misunderstanding of the idea of "elementary" in Eusebius. Theophilus is not writing to someone open and curious about becoming a Christian; he is engaged in an intellectual battle with someone who is philosophically hostile towards Christianity. Carl Curry has proposed that the genre is primarily "theogony," though this is far too specific and does not take into account the full argument of Theophilus or his specific stated purposes. Curry, "The Theogony of Theophilus," 318–26.

53. Cf. Young, "The Rhetorical Schools and Their Influence on Patristic Exegesis," 182–99.

54. Parsons, *Ancient Apologetic Exegesis*, ch. 4.

55. Parsons, *Ancient Apologetic Exegesis*.

Theophilus' World and Life

According to Parsons, the rhetorical context of AA is seen in two ways. First, the general structure of each book follows a particular rhetorical structure.[56] The book begins with an introduction (προοίμιον *prooimion; prooemium*) that establishes the main purpose (*hypothesis*) of the work. Then, there is a brief narrative (διήγησις *diēgēsis; narrativa*) that relates the context of the disagreement between the two parties and the main question that is up for debate (*quaestio*). After the introduction and narrative, then enters the section of proof (πίστις; *pistis*) or defense (the examination and cross examination of textual witnesses). The book, like other rhetorical works of this time, then ends with the conclusion (*peroratio*) which consists generally of a brief recapitulation of the arguments and purpose.[57]

Second, this rhetorical context is seen in the nature of the arguments in the proof section. Parsons analyzes how the rhetorical nature of the arguments used are in accord with major ancient rhetorical textbooks like that of Aristotle and Cicero. When analyzing witnesses, in this case textual witnesses, there are three main arguments common in ancient rhetoric for proving their truthfulness: "(1) discoursing on their 'authority' (*auctoritatem*), (2) discoursing on their 'witness of mode of life' (*vitam testium*), (3) discoursing on their 'consistency of testimony' (*constantiam testimoniorum*)."[58] On the other hand, in the time of cross examination, Cicero proposed these challenging arguments:

1. discoursing on their "foul mode of life" (*vitae turpitudinem*),
2. discoursing on their "inconsistency of testimony" (*testimoniorum inconstantiam*), or by
3. showing that what witnesses claim to have happened either could not have happened or
4. showing that it did not happen, or
5. showing that they could not have known, or
6. showing that they speak out of partiality.[59]

---

56. See Appendix 1 for a possible outline of the structure of Theophilus' work.

57. It is beyond the scope of this book to prove the common use of this rhetorical structure, but the reader may find such proof in Parsons, *Ancient Apologetic Exegesis*, ch. 4, where he gives several examples in sources like Philo and others, and then gives a detailed analysis of the structure in each book of AA.

58. Parsons, "By One and the Same Spirit," 40.

59. Parsons, "By One and the Same Spirit," 41.

All of these arguments are seen in AA and they all lay behind what he says about the nature of Scripture. There is one other argument that he uses not in this list, and that is the antiquity of the Scriptures. However, this is used to support the authority (defense argument 1) and the consistency (defense argument 3) of the Scriptures, and it also protects the Scriptures from the charge that what they say could not have been known by them (challenging argument 5).

Influence

From the later patristic writings, it is clear that Theophilus was not as influential as other second-century apologists, most notably Justin. However, he did have some influence shortly after his own time. Most notably, Tertullian used his works in his *Apology* (ca. AD 197), *Against Marcion*, and *Against Hermogenes*. Also, Irenaeus made use of Theophilus, especially his books one and two, which were likely produced at some point earlier than the third.[60] Lactantius also cites him, along with references in Cyril of Jerusalem and others. As mentioned before, his work was known to Eusebius and Jerome in the fourth and fifth centuries. At the end of the Patristic period, he is also used by John of Damascus. Therefore, Theophilus did have some measure of influence after his time in other Orthodox writers.

AA was copied in a collection with other patristic works by Gregory of Nyssa, Eusebius, Origen, Aenas, and Zacharias in the 10th or 11th centuries. This manuscript (Codex Marcianus gr. 496: 160 verso185 recto) was later taken to Venice in 1468 where it has become the best independent witness to Theophilus' AA that we currently possess.[61] We also possess another manuscript of the third book that is included in a collection of treatises on the Trinity from 1540. It is kept at the *Bibliothèque nationale* in Paris (Cod. Paris. G. 887).[62]

---

60. Loofs, *Theophilus von Antiochen Adversus Marcionem*, 44–80. Cf. Grant, "The Problem of Theophilus," 196.

61. Grant, "The Textual Tradition of Theophilus of Antioch," 146–150. Cf. Grant, "Introduction" in *Theophilus of Antioch*, xix–xxi.

62. Grant, "Introduction," in *Theophilus of Antioch*, xix–xx. Grant says that it was likely that the scribe accidentally copied the third book when he had intended to copy the second, since the second more explicitly refers to the divine *triad* and the generation of the *Logos* and *Sophia*.

Theophilus' World and Life

Having seen the world and life of Theophilus, and given a brief introduction to the date, purpose, style, and later use of AA, it is now fitting to put Theophilus in his modern scholarly context.

2

Theophilus in Recent Research

THOUGH THE AVERAGE EVANGELICAL knows very little about Theophilus and may have never heard of him, Theophilus has been at the center of various academic debates over the nature of Christian doctrine and the development of the Christian canon. This chapter will summarize the major trends in the study of Theophilus of Antioch. There are three main areas of the thought of Theophilus of Antioch that have received varied attention over the past 150 years: his Christology, trinitarianism, and use of Scripture.

THEOPHILUS ON CHRISTOLOGY

With respect to his Christology, the studies have been rather negative, beginning with the 1975 article by J. Bentivegna on a "Christianity without Christ by Theophilus of Antioch."[1] As the name indicates, Bentivegna claims that Theophilus defends Christianity without ever explicitly mentioning the name of Christ; even when he seeks to give an explanation for the name "Christian," he refers to the idea of anointing (*chrestus*) and not Christ.[2] This article goes on to claim that because of the apparent absence

---

1. Bentivegna, "A Christianity without Christ by Theophilus of Antioch," 107–30.
2. Grant, *Theophilus of Antioch*, I.1, 12. One interesting aspect of this connection is that the Roman historian Seutonius seems to have possibly mixed up the names of

of Christ from AA, Christ must not have played a major role in the overall thinking of the apologist.

Robert Grant has contributed various articles and book chapters to Theophilus. With respect to his Christology, Grant's position has developed over the years. In his 1950 article, "The Problem of Theophilus," Grant shows the strong Jewish context of the Christianity of Theophilus, even saying that "he was very close to what the later fathers called the school of Ebion."[3] Later in the same article, Grant refers to him as a "dynamistic monarchian Judaizer."[4] His Jewishness is defended by an appeal to his dependence on the Old Testament, lack of reference to Christ as the savior of the world, and his emphasis on law. Therefore, Grant has concluded that he has a view of Jewish-Christianity where Christ may be no more than an inspired prophet, who proclaims a law-based salvation.[5] This position has turned Theophilus into a case study for the broad diversity that was present in the early church, in support of the opinion of Walter Bauer.[6] However, Grant later moderated this position in his 1988 book on *The Greek Apologists*, merely identifying his form of Christianity as one developed in an

---

Cristus and *Crestus* [*Claudius*, 25.4], maybe this passage indicates a more widespread misunderstanding that Theophilus is using polemically. Similar silences on the person of Christ can be seen in the apologetic works of Athenagoras, Tatian, and Minucius Felix. However, with respect to Tatian, there are more extant works that help to clarify his understanding of Christ. Cf. Grant, *Greek Apologists*, 165.

3. Grant, "The Problem of Theophilus," 180.

4. Grant, "The Problem of Theophilus," 196.

5. Kruger gives a helpful observation on the use of the term "Jewish-Christian" that may indicate a problem that also lies behind the negative views of Theophilus' theology: "[this term] leaves unclear whether one has to be ethnically Jewish to be regarded as a Jewish Christian or whether one just needs to follow Jewish practices (or both). The problems with this definition are also exacerbated by the obvious overlap between Judaism and Christianity. . . . From one perspective, *all* Christianity is Jewish since it follows a Jewish messiah. Nevertheless, the term 'Jewish Christianity' still has a broad usefulness as a way to describe Christ-believers who maintained a 'faithful adherence to the law.'" Kruger, *Christianity at the Crossroads*, 115. Cf. Taylor, "The Phenomenon of Early Jewish-Christianity: Reality or Scholarly Invention?" 313–334; Malina, "Jewish Christianity or Christian Judaism," 46–57.

6. Bauer, *Heresy and Orthodoxy*; Ehrman, *Lost Christianities*. For a helpful critique of this theory as presented by Bauer and Ehrman, see Köstenberger and Kruger, *The Heresy of Orthodoxy*. Grant likewise affirms, "The existence of Theophilus as bishop of Antioch proves conclusively the indistinctness of the line between orthodoxy and heresy in the late second century, as well as of the line between Judaism and Christianity." Grant, "The Problem of Theophilus," 192.

area with a high influence of rabbinic and Hellenistic Judaism.[7] In this work, he also appears to recognize that the claim that Theophilus was a heterodox example of the "school of Ebion" does not stand up to the evidence of how he is seen and used by later orthodox writers.[8]

The translator of the academic version of *AA* in Spanish, José Pablo Martin, also has contributed a few articles to this discussion by seeing many similarities with Hellenistic Judaism in Theophilus, especially Philo. He says that his understanding of the Scriptures and the Logos are Philonic in all respects except for his exegesis.[9]

In response to Grant, William Schöedel seeks to show the suspect nature of Grant's affirmations about Theophilus' Christology. He highlights three main arguments that warrant reconsideration: (1) his influence on Irenaeus and the recognition of his orthodoxy by Eusebius and Jerome who had access to more of his writings,[10] (2) the questionable nature of Grant's claims about the Jewish-Christian context of Antioch at that time, (3) and the use of the Gospels and Pauline literature in Theophilus, especially the use of John in his defense of his idea of the Logos.[11]

The critique of Schoedel is targeted more at Grant's earlier work, since his extensive treatment of Theophilus in his 1988 book, *The Greek Apologists of the Second Century*, seems to be more positive towards the orthodoxy of Theophilus. In a way, he even anticipates Schoedel's critique when he says, "His 'mainstream' position is confirmed, at least in part, when both Irenaeus and Novatian occasionally use his work and excerpts appear in John of Damascus."[12] However, he later says that "the saving work of Christ disappears" from Theophilus and that he probably considered him as merely one of the prophets, something found in later writers like Marcellus of Ancyra and Paul of Samosata.[13]

---

7. Grant, *Greek Apologists*, 146, 165–167.

8. Grant, *Greek Apologists*, 146.

9. Martin, "Filón Hebreo y Teofilo Cristiano," 147–177

10. This point has particular force against Grant's claim that Theophilus was close to being an Ebionite, since Irenaeus knew of the Ebionites and considered them among the heretics like the docetists. He says that God "will judge also the Ebionites; how can they be saved unless it was God who wrought out their salvation upon earth? Or how shall man pass into God, unless God has [first] passed into man?" (*Against the Heresies*, 4.33.4); Cf. Kruger, *Christianity at the Crossroads*, 115.

11. Schöedel, "Theophilus of Antioch: Jewish Christian?" 279–97.

12. Grant, *The Greek Apologists*, 146.

13. Grant, *The Greek Apologists*, 172–3.

Another prominent Theophilus scholar, Rick Rogers, has addressed the Christological question in his book-length work on Theophilus. He proposes that the lack of emphasis on Jesus Christ is due to his genre. He helpfully identifies the genre of AA as protreptic and says that it presents a distinctly protreptic theology, as opposed to his ecclesiastical passion-based theology.[14] However, he still maintains that Theophilus has a catechetical and soteriological purpose, which lays the foundation for the presentation of his nomos-based soteriology. Due to this, he describes Theophilus in these words, "I think it might be better to say that Theophilus was a heterodox theologian, who upheld the conservative Christianity of Antioch."[15] This point led William Weinrich to say, "Bentivegna's claim of a 'Christianity without Christ' in Theophilus remains, and Rogers' thesis of a protreptic theology is wholly incapable of overcoming it."[16]

More recently, Parsons has sought to take on this challenge by emphasizing the importance of understanding and fully appreciating the protreptic style that also provides the basis of Rogers' argument. Parsons says that because of Theophilus's style, he intentionally seeks to leave soteriology out of the question. He compares the portion of Theophilus' theology that we find in AA to the elementary principles of Hebrews 6:1–2. Understanding this rhetorical structure and context is key in fully appreciating what Theophilus left out and why he emphasized what he did. In light of the limited evidence and the particular genre of what we do have of Theophilus, Parsons thus proposes an agnostic position towards his Christology.[17] Even Grant recognizes that Theophilus is not alone among the Greek Apologists in leaving out explicit references to the work of Christ and says that it is possibly "due to apologetic convention" and not necessarily due to a faulty theology.[18]

---

14. Rogers, *Theophilus of Antioch*, 165. Cf. Rogers, "Theophilus of Antioch," 218.

15. Rogers, "Theophilus of Antioch," 223. The seeming contradiction of this phrase may be due to the two classes of theology that Rogers finds in Theophilus, his protreptic soteriology and his ecclesiological.

16. Weinrich, "*Theophilus of Antioch: Life and Thought of a Second-Century Bishop* (review)," 603.

17. Parsons, *Ancient Apologetic Exegesis*, ch. 2.

18. Grant states, "Among the other early apologists, Athenagoras and Tatian also refrain from mentioning Jesus, while a little later Minucius Felix offers even more mysterious silences.... Perhaps the silence about Jesus is due to apologetic convention, perhaps to Theophilus' peculiar doctrine about Christ." Grant, *Greek Apologists*, 165. Though the possibility of a "peculiar doctrine about Christ" remains since we do not have access to Theophilus' explicit teaching on Christ. However, the fact that various apologists of the second century echo this same silence should lead to greater reserve in heterodox reconstructions of Theophilus' doctrine.

THEOPHILUS ON THE TRINITY

With regard to his view of the Trinity, there is a clear theology of the Logos in Theophilus. He uses the Logos in order to explain how God can be seen or be said to walk. Also, the Logos is connected with the Sophia and Spirit of God, though the distinction between the two is sometimes lacking in clarity. The first three days of creation are seen as types of the *triad*—God, Logos, and Sophia. However, because of the lack of an explicit reference to Christ or a union of the Logos with the incarnate Christ, and the fact that there is the appearance of a connection with man to this triad, many seek to throw out the trinitarianism of Theophilus. Of course, one must keep in mind the lack of clarity that is to be expected from a writer 150 years before Nicaea.

For example, Rogers says that it is wrong to consider him a precursor to Nicaea, or among the early proponents of Trinitarianism. He says, "He is not trinitarian or intentionally the initiator of trinitarian ideas."[19] However, Parsons has levelled a powerful argument against this view. He argues that it is appropriate to see that at least a trinitarian framework informs his use of threeness (triad) in reference to the Godhead. In light of the early, not-fully-developed affirmations of the Trinity in Justin and Athenagoras, it is fitting to see that a distinctly Christian and pre-Nicene trinitarian interpretation shapes his approach to certain passages like Genesis 1:26. Parsons recognizes that Rogers is right to say that Theophilus is not initiating trinitarian ideas (since these ideas are found in other second-century writers as well, such as Athenagoras[20]), though he is the first to use the term *triad*. However, he affirms that Rogers is mistaken for removing all trinitarian thought from Theophilus' theology.[21]

THEOPHILUS ON SCRIPTURE

The final area of research, which is closer to the topic of this book, is his view of Scripture. In 1861, Karl Otto produced a new and better edition of Theophilus's work, using the Venice manuscript as a basis. He also gave a helpful contribution to the study of his use of Scripture by providing a list of allusions and showing the significance of understanding scriptural

---

19. Rogers, *Theophilus*, 78.
20. Athenagoras, "Plea for the Christians," in ANF 2:133–4; ch. 10.
21. Parsons, "Very Early Trinitarian Expressions," 151.

allusions in Theophilus.[22] A second 19th-century scholar, Adolf von Harnack, also sought to address Theophilus's use of Scripture. He applies his distinction between "inspired writings" and "Scripture" to the writing of Theophilus and affirms that Theophilus considered the Old Testament as "Scripture" and "inspired," but the works that he cites from the New are only "inspired" and not explicitly grouped into the category of "Scripture" with the Old.[23]

Grant has also contributed several articles on this subject. In one article, he discusses the textual tradition that Theophilus used in his various Scripture citations.[24] Later in the same article he addresses the content of Scripture, and specifically looks at what books of the New Testament he knew and recognized. This study was directly targeted at the claims of Harnack. According to Grant's study, Theophilus recognized at least 12–15 of the New Testament writings (the Gospels—at least Matthew, Luke and John—, Acts, Paul's Epistles with the Pastorals, and the Apocalypse cited in his book *Against Hermogenes* and mentioned by Eusebius), and saw them as Scripture, though possibly less authoritative than the Old Testament. He makes this claim of a potentially inferior authority of the New Testament writings on the basis of his primarily Jewish reconstruction of Theophilus' theology.[25]

Manlio Simonetti also followed suit with an article in 1972 where he demonstrates how Theophilus saw the New Testament as "divine words." He affirms,

> [I]n fact, after Polycarp, Theophilus is the oldest author, inasmuch as he is only a little before Irenaeus who was influenced by him, who considers the writings of the New Testament, including in them not only the Gospels but also the Pauline Epistles, perfectly along the same line of inspiration and normality that the writings of the Old Testament had for Christians and Jews.[26]

---

22. Otto, "Gebrauch neutestamentlicher Schriften bei Theophilus von Antiochien," 617–22.

23. Von Harnack, "Theophilus von Antiochien und das Neue Testament," 1–21. This argument will become important in a later contribution.

24. Grant, "The Bible of Theophilus of Antioch," 173–96.

25. Grant, "Scripture, Rhetoric and Theology in Theophilus," 33–45.

26. Simonetti, "La Sacra Scrittura in Teofilo D'Antiochia," 197–207, at 197. Translation by the author.

With this statement, Simonetti has contributed to the development of the thesis of this book. However, Parsons points out that the major weakness of this work is its failure to give a detailed analysis of Theophilus's references to Scripture, which was due to length restraints. To fix such a problem, Parsons has provided a much more thorough look at the use of Scripture in Theophilus.[27] His stated purposes is "None of these older studies constituted a comprehensive, monograph length overview of Theophilus' use of the inspired texts. In the hope of filling this gap in the research, the present study is offered."[28] The research of his dissertation was later published in book form in 2005.[29]

Not only does he give a more detailed look at the explicit references to Scripture in Theophilus, but, in light of modern research on the power of allusions and ancient rhetoric, he also shows the underlying scriptural framework for his apology. Also, he seeks to correct the study of Theophilus and Scripture in light of a more complex understanding of patristic exegesis than just the simple terms of "allegorical" or "literal" interpretation.[30] His dissertation focuses on proving three points:

> [1] First, Theophilus of Antioch used the inspired texts to build rich inter-textual webs which focus his reader on traditional motifs of early Christian apology set in a Gentile milieu. [2] Second, he marshaled ancient reading strategies, Hellenistic philosophy and forensic rhetoric, in conjunction with his exegesis and use of inspired writings. [3] Third, he respected the details of the text and creatively interpreted them, but also followed particular exegetical traditions.[31]

However, Parsons does not develop the doctrine of Scripture in Theophilus, nor does he fully discuss Theophilus' use of non-canonical works, especially the Sibyl. This is particularly important in light of a recent book written by Craig Allert, *A High View of Scripture?*.[32] Though Allert does not address Theophilus specifically, he does level a general critique against traditional approaches to understanding the early church's doctrine of Scripture and inspiration. Allert summarizes his critique in these words,

---

27. Parsons and Bingham, "'By One and the Same Spirit,'" 8.
28. Parsons and Bingham, "By One and the Same Spirit," 10.
29. Parsons, *Ancient Apologetic Exegesis*.
30. Parsons, "By One and the Same Spirit," 35.
31. Parsons, "By One and the Same Spirit," 51.
32. Allert, *A High View of Scripture?*.

First, these treatments are selective in citing the evidence. Most show little concern for any sustained presentation on any church father, which betrays a rather simplistic presentation, unconcerned with the way Scripture functioned in the early church. Second, these treatments assume that any reference in the fathers to inspiration or truth automatically assumes an understanding of inspiration and inerrancy akin to the verbal plenary view. This occurs even when most admit that the fathers really give no detailed doctrine of Scripture. Third and most applicable to my point here, these treatments work from within the framework established by Zahn and especially Harnack, which causes them to have a foundational misconception about the evidence used to prove their point. In this framework, they place vital importance on the way documents are cited (or alluded to).[33]

One of the main areas of selectivity that he points out is the failure to recognize claims of inspiration applied to books or writers that the traditional evangelical would not identify as Scripture. Thus, Allert returns to the distinction between inspiration and Scripture made by Harnack and seeks to show that the early church had an understanding of inspiration that was broader than their concept of Scripture.[34]

Another important argument that Allert and Williams make is how though we cannot speak of a canon of Scripture formally in the second century, it was common to hear talk of a canon or rule of faith. Therefore, they claim that the Scriptures as a rule did not precede the summarized form of the church's teaching, and even Scripture had to be subjected and judged by that rule.[35] These critiques have been the primary impetus behind this book. For this reason, this book seeks to provide such a "sustained presentation" of Theophilus, to consider what he means by inspiration, and to see if he would have assigned the same authority to non-canonical books as he does to those that later came to be formally recognized as canonical.

In conclusion, this book seeks to contribute to the study of Theophilus by primarily looking at his use of Scripture and his affirmations about Scripture and what these reveal about his doctrine of Scripture. Before analyzing the role of Scripture in Theophilus' apology, it is important to first see the overall structure of his argument, which will also serve as an introduction to the basic principles that formed the foundation of his theology and worldview.

---

33. Allert, *A High View of Scripture?*, 71.
34. Allert, *A High View of Scripture?*, 58–60.
35. Allert, *High View of Scripture?*, 121–6; Williams, *Evangelicals and Tradition*, 47–102.

3

Theophilus' Apologetic for the Christian Worldview

THE APOSTLE PETER COMMANDS Christians as they live in the midst of a hostile world to "[S]anctify Christ as Lord in your hearts, always being prepared to make a defense to anyone who asks you for a reason for the hope that is in you" (1 Pet 3:15).[1] Theophilus provides a good example of this type of biblical apologetic. He approaches the apologetic task fully convinced of the truths of Scripture, delighting in the privilege of being called by the name of "Christian." From book 1, he seeks to remain faithful to his Christian commitment as he defends his faith. As he says, "[Y]ou call me a Christian as if I were bearing an evil name, I acknowledge that I am a Christian. I bear this name beloved of God in the hope of being useful to God. It is not the case, as you suppose, that the name of God is offensive."[2]

Not only is his apologetic method founded on a full commitment to God—his sovereign monarch—, he also seeks to base his entire worldview on Scripture—the revelation of his God. The Scriptures are the ultimate source of his worldview and thus for him the ultimate source of truth. Though his interpretation should be understood in light of his polemic and

1. All direct Scripture quotations are taken from *The Holy Bible: English Standard Version* (Wheaton, IL: Crossway Bibles, 2016).

2. Grant, *Theophilus of Antioch*, I.1.

at times an anti-heretical context,³ his goal is to submit himself to God's revelation in Scripture. It is this point that the rest of the book will seek to demonstrate. This chapter, however, seeks to give a more general understanding of his apologetic method and the key beliefs underlying his worldview—his presuppositions—, while the remaining chapters of the book will consider the essential role Scripture plays in his defense of Christianity.

Theophilus' primary apologetic purpose is to establish the superiority of the Christian system and demonstrate the inconsistency and falsehood of the pagan worldview held by Autolycus and others in the Greco-Roman world. This is the very nature of the protreptic genre in which he chose to write his apology; as Rogers has pointed out: "[T]he Greek literary genre, *protrepsis*, which was practiced by orators in the political arena and used by Aristotle and the Sophists, was designed to recruit students to join a school or to accept a set of teachings as normative for their lives . . . Protrepsis is the proper category for Theophilus' *To Autolycus*."⁴ With this in mind, his apologetic method becomes clearer through an analysis of (1) his positive development of a Christian worldview, (2) his understanding of the natural man, and (3) his presentation of the superiority of Christianity to all other philosophies and religions.

Theophilus does not fall into that temptation that some modern apologists have called "intellectual respectability."⁵ Due to the pressures of marginalization and persecution, it may have been natural for some Greek apologists to highlight similarities between Greek and Christian thought and thus show that Christianity was not as profane and criminal as was often alleged. Though at times he recognizes the strengths of certain philosophical systems, such as Plato and the Stoics,⁶ Theophilus always differs from them in key, worldview-shaping ways and shows their inconsistency in comparison with the scriptural system. Rather than making a synthesis between Greek philosophy and Christianity, his main argument is that, as a system of thought and way of life, Christianity is superior to all other worldviews and is actually the only one that is consistent with itself and

---

3. Cf. Grant, *The Greek Apologists*, 157–162.

4. Rogers, "Theophilus of Antioch," 218.

5. Frame, *A History of Western Philosophy and Theology*, 90–3.

6. For a presentation of possible Platonic influence, mediated through Philo of Alexandria, see Martin, "Filón Hebreo y Teófilo Cristiano," 301–17. For a presentation of possible Stoic influences, see McVey, "Use of Stoic Cosmogony," 32–58

with reality; and, far from being neutral, he sees all other systems as antithetical to Christianity.

A CHRISTIAN WORLDVIEW

The first key aspect of his apologetic method is his positive presentation of the Christian worldview. A person's worldview is the set of basic beliefs or presuppositions that form the lens through which that person understands and interprets the world. Developing the worldview apologetic of Greg Bahnsen, Gary DeMar defines a worldview in these terms: "A worldview is a network of presuppositions (which are not verified by the procedures of natural science) regarding reality (metaphysics), knowing (epistemology), and conduct (ethics) in terms of which every element of human experience is related and interpreted."[7] As DeMar states, there are three basic questions that any worldview must be able to answer: (1) the question of being—metaphysics or ontology, (2) the question of knowledge—epistemology, (3) and the question of right and wrong—ethics.[8] The answers to these questions then form the elementary principles or the basic presuppositions of the system. These beliefs are used to interpret the world and to guide the beliefs and practice of the adherent, and they are in a sense non-negotiable. Though Theophilus does not use the modern term "worldview," he frequently refers to the general idea of "truth." "Truth" for Theophilus is what the honest inquirer must search after, and he affirms that it is only found when one receives the divine teaching by faith. As we will see, he conceives of truth as a comprehensive understanding of the nature of God, man, the world, and a righteous conduct.

Theophilus develops the Christian worldview's teaching on all of these questions, shows Scripture's perfect harmony on all of these points, and shows the inconsistency and foolishness of the philosophers and poets in their attempts to answer these questions. Towards the end of his apology, Theophilus gives this summary of the key components of his worldview, which he invites Autolycus to adopt and which he holds forth as the standard by which all philosophers must be judged: "We acknowledge a God, but only one, the Founder and Maker and Demiurge of this whole universe. We know that everything is governed by providential care, but by him alone. We have learned a holy law, but we have as legislator the real

---

7. DeMar, *Pushing the Antithesis*, 42–43.
8. Frame, *Apologetics*, 32. Cf. Johnson, *The Absurdity of Unbelief*, ch. 5.

God, who teaches us to practice justice and piety and beneficence."[9] In this brief quote we begin to see his basic answers to the question of ontology, epistemology, and ethics. The basics of his ontology is a submission to the one true God who is the Creator and Sustainer of the whole creation. The basics of his epistemology is that truth is taught by God to those who believe and obey. The basics of his ethics is that one must submit to the holy law revealed by the one Creator God. The following sections of this chapter will summarize his answers to these worldview questions and the role they play in his apology.

Ontology

Theophilus develops a scriptural ontology consisting of three major presuppositions: (1.) the *monarchy* of God, (2.) the Creator-creature distinction, and (3.) divine providence. According to Theophilus, these are the three main ontological presuppositions that are essential to a consistent worldview. These main points can also be seen in the summary of his worldview quoted above, "We acknowledge a god, [1] but only one, [2] the Founder and Maker and Demiurge of this whole universe. [3] We know that everything is governed by providential care, but by him alone."[10]

Theophilus affirms that the philosophers either denied one or all of these points, or, when they did make certain propositions about them, they failed to be consistent with them.[11] Also, Theophilus seeks to demonstrate how these three presuppositions are found consistently throughout all of Scripture without any contradiction.

Divine Monarchy

His first ontological presupposition is "the sole rule of God" (μοναρχία; *monarchia*).[12] With this terminology, Theophilus has in mind two main ideas. First, he is demonstrating that the God of Christianity is the *one and only* God (*singularitatis*). There is not a multitude of gods but one. This point is presented in light of the foolishness of the tales of the gods and

---

9. Grant, *Theophilus of Antioch*, III.9.
10. Grant, *Theophilus of Antioch*, III.9.
11. Cf. Grant, *Theophilus of Antioch*, II.38, III.3, 7.
12. Grant, *Theophilus of Antioch*, II.8.

their immorality and how many of them were once men.[13] Also, he shows how the details of the Creation account ensure with clarity that there is only one God who is responsible for the creation of the whole world, including man and woman. In fact, it was the devil himself who first introduced the gross error of a belief in multiple gods when he seduced Adam and Eve with the possibility of themselves becoming gods (Gen 3:5).[14]

Secondly, this terminology carries the idea of lordship. This idea forms the basis of his epistemology and ethics as well. He says, "Only the real God who made the universe is to be worshipped, with holiness of heart and a sincere mind."[15] God is lord, and man, as his creature, must submit to him and worship him alone. As he says, "He is Lord because He is master of the universe, Father because he is before the universe, Demiurge and Maker because He is creator and maker of the universe, Most High because he is above everything, Almighty because he controls and surrounds everything."[16]

Though essential to his thought is the oneness of God, it is not the oneness found in Platonic or Aristotelian thought. Theophilus' conception of God is necessarily Trinitarian, or at least *triadic*: though it appears with the clarity to be expected of an ante-Nicene father. As has been noted, many modern scholars try to remove Theophilus from the development of ante-Nicene trinitarianism, but from various affirmations that Theophilus makes, we must agree with Parsons that there is a trinitarian framework that undergirds his understanding of God and creation.[17] He recognizes the hypostatic diversity of the one divine essence and speaks of it specifically in terms of threeness. Theophilus is actually the first writer to use the Greek version of the word for Trinity, τριάς (*trias*), though he uses it as though it had been used for some time before him.[18] He defines it this way, "the triad [Trinity] of God and his Logos and his Sophia."[19] He even understands the divine deliberation that preceded the creation of man in Genesis 1:26 to be inter-Trinitarian: "But he said 'Let us make' to none other than his own

---

13. Grant, *Theophilus of Antioch*, II.34.
14. Grant, *Theophilus of Antioch*, II.28.
15. Grant, *Theophilus of Antioch*, II.35.
16. Grant, *Theophilus of Antioch*, I.4.
17. Parsons, "Very Early Trinitarian Expressions," 151.
18. Schaff, *History of the Church*, 2:733.
19. Grant, *Theophilus of Antioch*, II.15.

Logos and his own Sophia."[20] He says that God created the world through his Logos and Sophia—"his two hands."[21] All of these ideas indicate that within this divine oneness there is also in some sense a divine threeness.

The Logos of God is the eternal Son of God. He eternally existed within God, being generated from him, not created.[22] As he says,

> What is the "voice" [Gen 3:8] but the Logos of God, who is also his Son?—not as the poets and mythographers describe sons of gods begotten of sexual union, but as the truth describes the Logos, always innate [λογος ενδιάθετος; *logos endiathetos*] in the heart of God [cf. Jn 1:18]. For before anything came into existence he had this as his Counsellor, his own Mind and Intelligence.... He did not deprive himself of the Logos but generated the Logos and constantly converses with his Logos.... [John the Apostle] shows that originally God was alone and the Logos was in him.... Since the Logos is God and derived his nature from God, whenever the Father of the universe wills to do so he sends him into some place where he is present and is heard and seen.[23]

This text demonstrates that this single divine being is God and Logos, Father and Son. In this quote, he affirms that the Logos was not a created being outside of God, for "he did not deprive himself of the Logos but generated the Logos and constantly converses with his Logos." He even claims that this "Logos is God," and that in some way the divine nature was communicated from God the Father to the Son. Though he does not explicitly connect the Logos with the incarnate Christ, it is possible that such an idea is in the background of his use of John 1:1–3 to defend the eternal existence of the Logos within the heart of God.[24]

The Sophia of God was the wisdom of God by which he made the world; and it was this wisdom, most likely one with the Holy Spirit, that revealed the secrets of God and creation to the prophets who were not there to witness it.[25]

---

20. Grant, *Theophilus of Antioch*, II.18.

21. Cf. Grant, *Theophilus of Antioch*, II.18; Schoedel, "Theophilus of Antioch," 283; Compton, "Theophilus of Antioch and Irenaeus on Logos and Sophia: The 'Two Hands of God.'"

22. Grant, *Theophilus of Antioch*, II.22.

23. Grant, *Theophilus of Antioch*, II.22. This affirmation is very similar to Athenagoras's statement in: Athenagoras, "Plea for the Christians," in ANF 2:133–134; ch. 10.

24. Grant, *Theophilus of Antioch*, II.22. Cf. Schoedel, "Theophilus of Antioch," 294.

25. Grant, *Theophilus of Antioch*, II.9–10.

Creator-Creature Distinction

The second main presupposition of Theophilus' system, like the presuppositional apologist Cornelius Van Til, is the Creator-Creature distinction.[26] If Theophilus had a chalkboard to use in his conversation with Autolycus, he probably would have begun in a way similar to professor Van Til by drawing two separate circles: one to indicate God and the other to represent creation. He says, "But what God is able to do is shown by this, that he first makes existent things out of the non-existent just as he wills. For the things impossible with men are possible with God [Luke 18:27]."[27] He rejects the philosophers who made creation eternal or part of God, affirming clearly the biblical teaching of a creation *ex nihilo*. For example, in II.4 he takes on the Platonists for their belief in an eternal creation:

> Plato and his followers acknowledge that God is uncreated, the Father and Maker of the universe; next they assume that uncreated matter is also God, and say that matter was coeval with God. But if God is uncreated and matter is uncreated, then according to the Platonists God is not the Maker of the universe, and as far as they are concerned the unique sovereignty [μοναρχία; *monarchia*] of God is not demonstrated. Furthermore, as God is immutable because he is uncreated, if matter is uncreated it must also be immutable, and equal with God; for what is created is changeable and mutable, while the uncreated is unchangeable and immutable. What would be remarkable if God made the world out of preexistent matter? Even a human artisan, when he obtains material from someone, makes whatever he wishes out of it. But the power of God is revealed by his making whatever he wishes out of the non-existent, just as the ability to give life and motion belongs to no one but God alone. For a man makes an image but cannot give reason or breath or sensation to what he makes, while God has this power greater than his: the ability to make a being that is rational, breathing, and capable of sensation. As in all these instances God is more powerful than man, so he is in his making and having made the existent out of the non-existent; he made whatever he wished in whatever way he wished.[28]

---

26. Cf. Van Til, *Defense of the Faith*, ch. 2: "It must be demonstrated to them that when we speak of reality, we at once make a distinction within it, namely the reality of God as self-sufficient and of the universe as existing by his plan, creation and providence."

27. Grant, *Theophilus of Antioch*, II.13. Irenaeus uses this same reference to Luke 18:27 and seems to even be dependent upon Theophilus here in *Against Heresies* 2.10.4.

28. Grant, *Theophilus of Antioch*, II.4; cf. II.8.

Theophilus repeatedly affirms that creation was out of nothing (*ex nihilo*) because before creation only God existed. He affirms this distinction by affirming plainly the biblical account of creation. He even affirms that this is the main point of the very first words of Scripture: "These are the first teachings which the divine Scriptures give. It indicates that the matter from which God made and fashioned the world was in a way created, having been made by God."[29] Not only do the Scriptures begin with this point, but all of the other parts of Scripture are consistent with this teaching: "In the first place, in complete harmony they [the prophets] taught us that he made everything out of the non-existent. For there was nothing co-eval with God; he was his own locus; he lacked nothing; he existed before the ages. He wished to make man so that he might be known; for him, then, he prepared the world."[30]

Divine Providence

The third major presupposition, also in a fashion similar to Van Til, is expressed as a belief in the comprehensive providence of God.[31] He denies the foolishness of the philosophers who affirmed the existence of chance or fate. He affirms that God did not simply create and let the world work on its own, rather God is active in sustaining the world through his providence.[32] This idea brings him full circle to the first presupposition that saw God as the only and supreme ruler of all things. For this reason, one's understanding of God, especially his lordship, must also shape one's ethics and epistemology.

Ethics

Theophilus is fully convinced that one's ethics not only determines the validity of a doctrine, but also that a proper ethic is necessary for true knowledge. In his mind, the answer to the question of ethics is intimately connected with the answer to the ontological question. The fact that God is the only true God and all of creation and man himself is his creation, man

---

29. Grant, *Theophilus of Antioch*, II.10.
30. Grant, *Theophilus of Antioch*, II.10.
31. Van Til, *Defense of the Faith*, ch. 7.5.
32. Grant, *Theophilus of Antioch*, II.8.

must submit to him. As mentioned above, his basic ontological principle is summarized in the *monarchy* of God, which has the ontological reality of God's exclusiveness, and the ethical reality of his lordship and claim to all of man's worship and service. It is for this reason that he did not abandon the world but gave a holy law.[33]

First, he shows that the pagan religions cannot be true because their so-called gods are full of adulteries, murders, and lies.[34] Second, as we will see more in the section on epistemology, true knowledge is ethical and soteriological; that is to say, man cannot really know God in his sin unless God does a salvific miracle in the soul of a man.[35] It is man's sinful state that makes him unable to see the truth of God that is revealed in all of creation or in his Word.[36] It is also the sin of the philosophers, along with demonic deception, that made them inconsistent with what glimmers of truth they were able to discover from creation.[37] However, the truth of God, creation, man, and judgment, "will be understood by everyone who seeks for the wisdom of God, and is pleasing to him through faith and righteousness and good deeds."[38]

He summarizes the Christian ethic in these words by which he characterizes the Christian community, "temperance is present, continence is exercised, monogamy is preserved, purity is guarded; injustice is driven out, sin is uprooted, righteousness is practised, law is the guiding principle, piety is preformed, God is acknowledged; truth controls, grace preserves, peace protects; holy Logos guides, Sophia teaches, Life controls, God reigns."[39] Here he clearly rebuts the frequent false accusations made against Christians and shows that their rule of life is the just law established by God himself. This ethical presupposition that he presents as the only true and consistent one is threefold: (1) God has revealed a holy law to be the rule of life; (2) God will hold all men to account for their deeds in the final judgment; and (3) this life is not where scores are settled, rather there is a future resurrection and day of judgement.

---

33. Grant, *Theophilus of Antioch*, II.34.
34. Grant, *Theophilus of Antioch*, I.9, III.5–8.
35. Grant, *Theophilus of Antioch*, I.7.
36. Grant, *Theophilus of Antioch*, I.7.
37. Grant, *Theophilus of Antioch*, II.12.
38. Grant, *Theophilus of Antioch*, II.38.
39. Grant, *Theophilus of Antioch*, III.15.

A Holy Law

First, he uses the Ten Commandments as the summary of the Christian ethic, referring to them as "the ten chapters of this great and marvelous law, which suffice for all righteousness."[40] This holy law is sufficient to rule one's relationship with God,[41] with foreigners,[42] how to respond to personal sin,[43] inter-personal relationships,[44] and with persecutors and the state.[45]

Proper ethics comes from submission to God's lordship and is necessary for a consistent system of thought. There is something amiss in our system if it is not accompanied with a good lifestyle. The first part of book 3 primarily seeks to demonstrate that the wickedness of which the Christians are accused—cannibalism, incest, and polygamy[46]—are actually true of the philosophers and pagans. He says, "We have learned a holy law, but we have as legislator the real God, who teaches us to practice justice and piety and beneficence."[47] In Christianity, obedience is not merely submitting to an abstract law, but it is submitting to the lordship or monarchy of the one true God. In this way, his ethical principles clearly flow from his ontological principles.

A Final Judgement and Resurrection

Second, he shows how the prophets are consistent in their teaching on the final judgment, and that even the Greek Sibyl and the poets and philosophers proclaimed this reality (though the philosophers at other times denied it).[48] He says, "[God] is the instructor of the godly and the father of the righteous, but the judge and punisher of the ungodly."[49] He therefore calls Autolycus to faith and holiness now, so that he will not be judged later: "If you will, you too must obey him and believe him, so that after disbelieving

---

40. Grant, *Theophilus of Antioch*, III.9.
41. Grant, *Theophilus of Antioch*, III.9.
42. Grant, *Theophilus of Antioch*, III.10.
43. Grant, *Theophilus of Antioch*, III.11.
44. Grant, *Theophilus of Antioch*, III.12–13.
45. Grant, *Theophilus of Antioch*, III.14.
46. Grant, *Theophilus of Antioch*, III.4.
47. Grant, *Theophilus of Antioch*, III.9.
48. Grant, *Theophilus of Antioch*, II.36–8.
49. Grant, *Theophilus of Antioch*, I.3.

now you will not be persuaded later, punished with eternal tortures."[50] It is only through submission to God's holy law that one is able to "escape the eternal punishments and be judged worthy of receiving eternal life from God."[51] In fact, the resurrection is how God undoes the curse of the Fall: "What man acquired for himself through his neglect and disobedience [seeking immortality], God now freely bestows upon him through love and mercy, when man obeys him."[52] Or in another place he says metaphorically, "Again, just as when some vessel has been fashioned and has some fault, and is resmelted or refashioned so that it becomes new and perfect, so it happens to man through death [due to his own sin]; for he has virtually been shattered so that in the resurrection he may be found sound, I mean spotless and righteous and immortal."[53]

It is here that recent scholars' claims about the intriguing absence of Christ and the Gospel in the writing of Theophilus has some weight.[54] It is noteworthy that when discussing the problem of sin and the necessity of obeying God's Law Theophilus does not point Autolycus immediately to the cross of Christ where the forgiveness of sin was obtained through his sacrificial death. However, this may also be due to his protreptic style in which he focuses more on establishing the elementary ethical principles of the Christian worldview which truly does establish righteousness (1 Jn 3:7) and holiness (1 Pet 1:15–16) as the will of God for Christians. The free grace of God given by faith alone is not incompatible with a desire to live a holy life submitted to God's Law; in fact, biblically speaking, it is the necessary fruit of that grace (cf. Eph 2:8–10). Also, Theophilus may have seen his goal as preparatory for the announcement of the good news of the Gospel to Autolycus. In a way, Theophilus seeks first to convince Autolycus that he is sick before providing him the full remedy.[55] There is a clear call to repentance,[56] but the call to believe in Christ as redeemer is curiously absent. His purpose appears to focus on convincing Autolycus of

---

50. Grant, *Theophilus of Antioch*, I.14.
51. Grant, *Theophilus of Antioch*, II.34, cf. I.8, 13, II.27.
52. Grant, *Theophilus of Antioch*, II.27.
53. Grant, *Theophilus of Antioch*, II.26.
54. Grant, "The Problem of Theophilus," 196; Bentivegna, "A Christianity without Christ by Theophilus of Antioch," 107–30.
55. Grant, *Theophilus of Antioch*, I.7.
56. Grant, *Theophilus of Antioch*, I.14.

his sinfulness and his need for God's grace, which sadly does not seem to have been achieved during the process of writing these three books.

The ethical question is both connected with the ontology question and the epistemological question. As the summary of his presuppositions indicates: "We have learned a holy law, but we have as legislator the real God, who teaches us to practise justice and piety and beneficence."[57] The true ethic comes from the revelation—epistemology—of the one true God and lord of all—ontology.

Epistemology

One of the clearest passages where Theophilus develops his understanding of epistemology is found in book 1, chapters 2–8. Here, Theophilus address three key elements of his epistemology: (1) the nature of revelation, (2) the inability of natural man, and (3) the true way we know God.

The Revelation of the Unseen God

Unlike the idols of Autolycus, the God of Theophilus cannot be seen with physical eyes. God is not seen or heard through the physical senses, but through the eyes and ears of the soul.[58] Because God is the maker, fashioner, and sustainer of all, he has revealed himself in the very existence of the world: "God made everything out of what did not exist, bringing it into existence so that his greatness might be known and apprehended through his works [cf. Rom 1:19–20]."[59] Though he is not seen sitting in a temple or represented in some image, he is known because "his providence and works" declare him.[60] Just like someone standing on the shore and looking at a ship off in the water; since he sees the boat heading for harbor in an intelligent direction, he is aware that there must be a captain.[61] This is similar to the cosmological argument that bases the need for a creator or designer in the reality of design and intention found in creation. And, in I.6, he gives a very thorough account of the works of God in providence,

---

57. Grant, *Theophilus of Antioch*, III.9.
58. Grant, *Theophilus of Antioch*, II.2.
59. Grant, *Theophilus of Antioch*, I.4.
60. Grant, *Theophilus of Antioch*, I.5.
61. Grant, *Theophilus of Antioch*, I.5.

including the reproduction of animals, the movement of the stars, and the bringing of storms and rains, all of which serve as a testimony to the wise guidance of God. All of these things are his works that declare him to be the God and Lord of all. Theophilus sees all of creation as the revelation of God, manifesting *that* he is and *who* he is. Since God is invisible and his appearance is too glorious for us to bear, we cannot fully comprehend him; but we can know him through revelation in his Word and in nature.

The Eyes of the Soul

However, though he recognizes that all men have soulish eyes by which they are able to perceive God, the natural man has these eyes blinded to the truth of God. As he says,

> For God is seen by those who are capable of seeing Him, once they have the eyes of the soul opened. All men have eyes, but some have eyes which are hooded by cataracts and do not see the light of the sun. Just because the blind do not see, however, the light of the sun does not fail to shine; the blind must blame themselves and their eyes. So you also, O man, have cataracts over the eyes of your soul because of yours sins and wicked deeds.
> Just as a man must keep a mirror polished, so he must keep his soul pure. When there is rust in the mirror, a man's face cannot be seen in it; so also when there is sin in a man such a man cannot see God.[62]

Therefore, though God can be clearly seen in Creation, and all of his works declare his name, the natural man in his sin is in general unable to discern the truth of God. It is not that man does not have the natural faculties necessary for knowing God, for "all men have eyes," but it is due to sin that man cannot see God. It is for this reason that man cannot see God, the truth of whom shines as brightly as the sun: "All this brings darkness upon you, just as when a flux of matter comes over the eyes and they cannot see the light of the sun. So also, O man, your ungodliness brings darkness upon you and you cannot see God."[63]

For this reason, though Autolycus had challenged him saying, "Show me your God," Theophilus turns the tables on him and says: "So show me yourself." It is Autolycus's own sin that makes him incapable of seeing

---

62. Grant, *Theophilus of Antioch*, I.2.
63. Grant, *Theophilus of Antioch*, I.2.

God. As he says, after listing several sins in which Autolycus was involved, "God does not become visible to those who do such things unless they first cleanse themselves from all defilement."[64]

Like Romans 1:18–22, Theophilus shows that man depends for his very existence and knowledge on God and his revelation, but due to his sin he still does not know the God who created him: "You speak of him, O man; you breathe his breath; you do not know him. This has happened to you because of the blindness of your soul and your heart, but if you will you can be cured. Deliver yourself to the physician, and he will couch the eyes of your soul and heart."[65]

For this reason, no manner of demonstration or miraculous confirmation will induce man to believe the truth. Just as the Lord Jesus said in Luke 16:31, if man does not believe the revelation of God that is all around him or contained in the Scriptures, he will not even believe if a miracle is performed. As Theophilus himself says, "Even if I were to show you a dead man raised and alive, you might perhaps disbelieve this. God has given you many indications for believing him."[66] The problem of man is not a knowledge problem, nor a problem with his access to knowledge about God, nor a problem of insufficient evidence; it is an ethical problem—a sin problem.

Faith and the Healing Physician

If this is the case of man in sin, what is the solution? How can man know God? The answer is two-fold. As a previous passage pointed out, man must first submit himself to the great physician if the blindness and deafness of his soul will be healed. "But before all, faith and the fear of God [Prov 1:7] must take the lead in your heart; then you will understand these things."[67] There must first be an ethical renovation worked in man; the great physician must first cure his blindness. If man will understand truth, he must begin with faith and submission to God's lordship: "Do you not know that faith leads the way in all actions?"[68] Again, we note the curious absence of a call to trust in Christ as the redeemer and forgiver of sins, but what he says is true to the scriptural witness though not as complete as one might expect.

---

64. Grant, *Theophilus of Antioch*, I.2.
65. Grant, *Theophilus of Antioch*, I.7.
66. Grant, *Theophilus of Antioch*, I.13.
67. Grant, *Theophilus of Antioch*, I.7.
68. Grant, *Theophilus of Antioch*, I.8.

Second, man must sit as the student of God's Logos and Sophia: "Who is the physician? He is God, who heals and gives life through his Logos and Sophia."[69] After having believed in God and sought to him for spiritual healing, the natural man may then be instructed by God, having the scales of his eyes removed. In the Scriptures, we have the direct revelation of God through the Spirit who reveals the truth of God to which our sins had blinded us. It is to this Word that Theophilus regularly calls Autolycus if he wants to understand truth.[70]

The state of man in sin was so desperate that it was even destined to completely destroy itself if God had not given special revelation. This shows the importance of submitting first of all to God's revelation. Theophilus compares the giving of divine revelation to the influx of the rivers into the ocean:

> And we say that for us the world is in the likeness of the sea. For just as the sea, if it did not have the flow of river and springs as a supply of nourishment, would long ago have been parched because of its saltiness, so also the world, if it had not had the law of God and the prophets flowing and gushing forth sweetness and compassion and righteousness and the teaching of God's holy commandments, would already now have failed, because of the evil and sin abounding in it.[71]

However, he continues his analogy. God has not only preserved the world through giving his Word, he has also helped sailors on their journey through the sea of this world by establishing local churches which help men to understand the truth. On the other hand, the philosophers and heretics are compared to pirates who fill their boats with riches but then crash into the rocky and inhabitable islands of false doctrine and are completely ruined by their errors.[72] Just as he said in another place, "The God and Father and Maker of the universe did not abandon mankind but gave a law and sent holy prophets to proclaim and to teach the human race, that each one of us might become sober and recognize that God is one."[73]

To demonstrate this point, Theophilus shares his own conversion story, and how it was not until he came to the Scriptures that he was truly

---

69. Grant, *Theophilus of Antioch*, I.7.
70. Grant, *Theophilus of Antioch*, I.14, II.38.
71. Grant, *Theophilus of Antioch*, II.14.
72. Grant, *Theophilus of Antioch*, II.14.
73. Grant, *Theophilus of Antioch*, II.34.

instructed in the truth of God. The revelation of God demands belief, and Autolycus is called to submit himself to the truth of God revealed in the Scriptures: "If you will, you too must reverently read the prophetic writings. They will be your best guides for escaping the eternal punishments and for obtaining the eternal benefits of God."[74]

THE NATURAL MAN

The second way that Theophilus stands out in his apologetic method is in his understanding of the natural man. As has been seen, the natural man has the revelation of God all around him; he cannot avoid it, like we cannot avoid the light of the sun. However, sin has blinded the eyes of his soul so that he cannot see God. Man, therefore, is in desperate need of a spiritual change in order to know God. But, Theophilus also recognizes, as the saying goes, even a blind squirrel may stumble upon an acorn: "except that sometimes, some poets, becoming sober in soul and departing from the demons, made statements in agreement with those of the prophets in order to bear witness to themselves and to all men concerning the sole rule of God and the judgement and the other matters they discussed."[75]

How does he account for the natural man being able to discern certain truths about God? As we have already seen, since the truth of God is all around, it actually takes an active work on behalf of man—sin—to blind his eyes to the truth. As Paul said, man is guilty of "suppressing the truth in unrighteousness" (Rom 1:18) and changing the truth of God for a lie (Rom 1:25). For this reason, Theophilus affirms that the small kernels of truth that can be found among the philosophers are due to what modern apologists have called "borrowed capital."[76] The truth shining through in the philosophers is due to the brightness and power of the truth, not the reason of the philosopher: "All of them said these things, for they were convinced by the truth."[77] He not only believes that in many cases the philosophers are directly borrowing from Scripture, since for him it forms the most ancient religion,[78] but he also states that though they may find a kernel of truth, they cannot be consistent with that truth nor can they fit it in a coherent

---

74. Grant, *Theophilus of Antioch*, I.14.
75. Grant, *Theophilus of Antioch*, II.8.
76. Bahnsen, *Presuppositional Apologetics*, 96.
77. Grant, *Theophilus of Antioch*, II.38.
78. Grant, *Theophilus of Antioch*, II.37–8.

system of thought, which can only be found in the biblical system revealed by God:

> To be sure, many writers have imitated it and have desired to compose a narrative about these matters [the scriptural account of creation], but, although they derived their starting-point from it in dealing with the creation of the world or the nature of man, what they said did not contain even a slight spark worthy of truth. What has been said by philosophers, historians, and poets is thought to be trustworthy because of its embellished style, but what they say is proved foolish and pointless by the abundance of their nonsense and the absence of even the slightest measure of the truth in their writings. Even if something true seems to have been proclaimed by them, it is mixed with error. Just as some deadly poison when mixed with honey or wine anything else makes the whole harmful and useless; so their loquacity is found to be pointless labour and causes harm to those who are persuaded by it.[79]

Moreover, not only do they fail to be consistent with the truth they have, they actually have a system that is hostile to the one true God. This is right in line with the affirmations of Romans 1:18–23:

> For the wrath of God is revealed from heaven against all ungodliness and unrighteousness of men, who by their unrighteousness suppress the truth. 19 For what can be known about God is plain to them, because God has shown it to them. 20 For his invisible attributes, namely, his eternal power and divine nature, have been clearly perceived, ever since the creation of the world, in the things that have been made. So they are without excuse. 21 For although they knew God, they did not honor him as God or give thanks to him, but they became futile in their thinking, and their foolish hearts were darkened. 22 Claiming to be wise, they became fools, 23 and exchanged the glory of the immortal God for images resembling mortal man and birds and animals and creeping things.

Also, John Calvin made a very similar affirmation when he said,

> Certainly I do not deny that one can read competent and apt statements about God here and there in the philosophers, but these always show a certain giddy imagination. As was stated above, the Lord indeed gave them a slight taste of his divinity that they might not hide their impiety under a cloak of ignorance. And sometimes he impelled them to make certain utterances by the confession of

---

79. Grant, *Theophilus of Antioch*, II.12.

which they would themselves be corrected. But they saw things in such a way that their seeing did not direct them to the truth, much less enable them to attain it! They are like a traveler passing through a field at night who in a momentary lightning flash sees far and wide, but the sight vanishes so swiftly that he is plunged again into the darkness of the night before he can take even a step—let alone be directed on his way by its help. Besides, although they may chance to sprinkle their books with droplets of truth, how many monstrous lies defile them![80]

Though man knows the true God because he has revealed himself in all of creation, even man's consciousness, the natural man cannot form a system that submits to God because he is hostile to him:

> ... [The philosophers] went astray and still go astray by speaking not of God but of pointless and useless matters. Thus they are eager to speak of Homer and Hesiod and the other poets, but they not only neglect but even slander the glory of the imperishable and only God; in addition, they have persecuted those who worship Him and do daily persecute them. ... Such men necessarily lost the wisdom of God and did not discover the truth.[81]

Therefore, what is the inquirer to do with the glimmers of truth that can be found in the teaching of the philosophers? He must submit to the lordship of God, holding his revelation as the supreme authority. Therefore, he cannot blindly accept the truth of philosophers since it is couched in a system whose presuppositions are contrary to those of the Christian worldview: "One must therefore pay attention and understand what is said, critically examining the remarks of philosophers and of poets as well."[82] They are like pearls in a pig's nose, or a castle built on a sandy foundation. We must be careful because though truth may be found, just a few pages away the same truth will be undermined by one of the falsehoods inherent in the system.

Like Romans 1, Theophilus attributes all idolatry and sin to a twisting and rejection of the truth of who God is. Sin and error are a deliberate rebellion against the reality of God: "The multitude of foolish men serve these [idols], but they reject the Maker and Fashioner of the universe and the Nourisher of all breath, in obedience to vain doctrines because of the

---

80. Calvin, *Institutes of the Christian Religion*, 1:277.
81. Grant, *Theophilus of Antioch*, III.30.
82. Grant, *Theophilus of Antioch*, III.7.

hereditary error of their unintelligent opinions."[83] It is for this reason that he can affirm the reality of general or natural revelation without seeking to create a natural theology. The truth shines brightly in creation, but because of sin man can only twist it or deny it. And for this rebellion, which is manifested in their hatred of the truth and persecution of Christians,[84] they will be judged.[85] As Romans 1:20 says, "so they are without excuse."

In his critique of paganism and presentation of the superiority of Christianity, he saw himself with a similar task to that of the prophets who: "suffered pangs, grieving over the godless race of mankind, and put to shame those who thought they were wise because of their error and hardness of heart [cf. Rom 1:22]."[86] In this passage he refers to the idolatry and false notions about God of the people that are strongly condemned by the prophets Isaiah, Jeremiah, and Hosea, and also by Deuteronomy and Psalms. He also alludes to Romans 1:22 in this chapter.

Later, in Book 3, he makes another allusion to Romans 1 when he says,

> Thus they are eager to speak of Homer and Hesiod and the other poets, but they not only neglect but even slander the *glory of the imperishable* and only *God*; in addition, they have persecuted those who worship and daily do persecute them. Moreover, they have appointed prizes and honours for those who euphoniously insult God, while they have stoned and killed those who are zealous for virtue and practise a holy life, and to this day they afflict them with cruel tortures [cf. Justin, *First Apology*, 49]. Such men necessarily lost the wisdom of God and did not discover the truth.[87]

Therefore, Theophilus recognizes the reality of truth and what theologians call common grace in the natural man, but he suffers the fate of inconsistency, practical negation, and rebellion if not submitted to the one and only monarch and his revelation of himself through his Logos and Sophia.

THE SUPERIORITY OF CHRISTIANITY

The final way that Theophilus stands out as a biblically consistent apologist is how he affirms the superiority of Christianity. In reference to this belief,

83. Grant, *Theophilus of Antioch*, II.34.
84. Grant, *Theophilus of Antioch*, III.30.
85. Grant, *Theophilus of Antioch*, I.8, 14.
86. Grant, *Theophilus of Antioch*, II.35.
87. Grant, *Theophilus of Antioch*, III.30.

Haykin says, "It was a conviction that was rooted in the New Testament and permeated the ancient church's witness to a sin-shaped culture."[88] Theophilus demonstrates that Christianity is the only consistent worldview, is the only worldview that derives directly from divine revelation, and is a much more ancient faith.

First, Theophilus points out that Christianity is the only logically coherent system of truth. Consistency is the test of a valid worldview.[89] He points out that it requires much greater faith to believe in man-made idols, than the one true God: "You believe that statues made by men are gods and work miracles. Then do you not believe that the God who made you can later make you over again [in the resurrection]?"[90] Not only does the Christian worldview actually provide the only viable explanation for the state of the world,[91] it is also the only worldview that is consistent: "For this reason it is plain that all the rest were in error, and that only the Christians have held the truth—we who are instructed by the Holy Spirit who spoke in the holy prophets and foretold everything."[92] The philosophers were all guilty of denying one another and even contradicting themselves.[93] But, the Scriptures in no place contradict but are all inspired by the one Spirit of God.

This leads to the second way in which Christianity is superior to all other religions. It is only Christianity that is based on direct revelation from God. As he says,

> The men of God, who were possessed by a holy spirit and became prophets and were inspired and instructed by God himself, were taught by God and became holy and righteous. . . . All of them were consistent with one another and with themselves, and they described events which had previously occurred, events in their own time, and events which are now being fulfilled in our times.[94]

It is from the Spirit's inspiration of the Scriptures that the Christian worldview derives its consistency: "One can see how consistently and harmoniously all the prophets spoke, having given utterance through one

---

88. Haykin, *Rediscovering the Church Fathers*, 85.
89. Johnson, *Absurdity of Unbelief*, loc. 1688–1697.
90. Grant, *Theophilus of Antioch*, I.8.
91. Grant, *Theophilus of Antioch*, II.23.
92. Grant, *Theophilus of Antioch*, II.33.
93. Grant, *Theophilus of Antioch*, III.3, 7.
94. Grant, *Theophilus of Antioch*, II.9.

and the same spirit concerning the unity of God, and the creation of the world, and the formation of man."[95] Unlike the Scriptures, which come from God through a pure spirit, Theophilus even attributes the doctrines of many of the philosophers to the inspiration, not of the Spirit of God, but of demons.[96] The work of demons and the sin of man are what lead to the inconsistency of all non-Christian worldviews. Though the pagan prophets claimed to depend on their gods: "How much more, then, shall we know the truth, since we learn it from the holy prophets, who were filled with the holy Spirit of God? For this reason, all the prophets spoke harmoniously and in agreement with one another when they predicted what was going to happen to the whole world."[97]

Third, Theophilus affirms the superiority of the Christian worldview because of its antiquity.[98] Not only do the earliest writings of Christianity, according to his chronology, precede any of the other religions, it is only Christianity that has the work of the Holy Spirit by which primeval history can reliably be made known to man.[99] The antiquity of Christianity forms the major part of the argument for the last part of book 3.[100] As McVey has pointed out, "Since he clearly assumes that the antiquity of the biblical account makes it a superior source of religious truth, the extensive chronological argument of the third book is essential to establishing his view."[101] Though Theophilus might have exaggerated the amount of direct borrowing that was being done by the pagan prophets, it is clear that he is so convinced of the superiority of Christianity that any truth found among the pagans can be attributed to a type intellectual theft.[102]

Therefore, Theophilus is not attempting to make Christianity appear intellectually respectable. His main purpose is to show the utter folly of the non-Christian worldview, to demonstrate how Christianity is superior, and to call Autolycus to repent of his sins and to submit his wandering and rebellious mind to the revelation of God in the Scriptures.

---

95. Grant, *Theophilus of Antioch*, II.35; cf. III.12.
96. Grant, *Theophilus of Antioch*, II.8.
97. Grant, *Theophilus of Antioch*, III.17.
98. Grant, *Theophilus of Antioch*, II.30, III.20, III.29.
99. Grant, *Theophilus of Antioch*, II.10.
100. Grant, *Theophilus of Antioch*, III.16–30.
101. McVey, "The Use of Stoic Cosmogony," 42
102. Grant, *Theophilus of Antioch*, II.37–8.

CONCLUSION

As has been demonstrated, Theophilus does not try to start on the same playing field as the pagan philosopher and then try to work upward to the truth of Christianity upon shared convictions. Rather, he is from the beginning firmly submitted to the truth of Christianity. For this reason, and in light of his understanding of the natural man, he realizes that what Autolycus needs most is not fanciful oratory or philosophical argumentations, but he needs a work of God in opening the eyes of his soul to see the truth. He recognizes that the success of his apology depends upon the miraculous work of God. This is evidenced in his explicit affirmations, and in a prayer with which he concludes his second book: "I ask favour from the only God that I may speak the whole truth exactly, in accordance with his will, so that you and every one who reads these books may be led by his truth and grace."[103]

---

103. Grant, *Theophilus of Antioch*, III.23. Haykin likewise points out that this is the first principle of Early Christian apologetic as demonstrated by *The Letter to Diognetus*: "First, there is the recognition of the vital importance of prayer. The author mentions right at the beginning of his treatise that he is praying for Diognetus's conversion. He is very aware that unless Diognetus is given ears to hear the truth, all efforts to write this treatise for him will be in vain." Haykin, *Rediscovering the Church Fathers*, ch. 3.

PART 2

Theophilus' Doctrine of Scripture

4

Theophilus' Bible

HAVING STUDIED THE BASIC tenets of Theophilus' thought and worldview and their importance for his overall argument, we now draw closer to the main purpose of this book of showing his understanding of Scripture. Prior to considering the explicit and implicit affirmations of Theophilus with regards to the nature of Scripture, it is important to first discuss how Theophilus uses the Scriptures and draw some preliminary lines of the books that he considered as Scripture. This book will often refer to New Testament and Old Testament writings because that is what they are to the modern reader. However, these terms themselves are somewhat anachronistic when applied to Theophilus. Likewise, the title of this chapter does not intend to imply that Theophilus possessed a complete one-volume book of Scripture called the Bible as it is often used today. This chapter will look briefly at the *status quo* of the Scriptures in the second century, and then will look specifically at the content and use of the Scriptures in Theophilus in particular.

SCRIPTURE AND CANON IN THE SECOND CENTURY

As Robert Wilken has said, the Bible was omnipresent in the early church.[1] However, we see this "omnipresence" in the diversity of practical contexts

---

1. Wilken, *The Spirit of Early Christian Thought.*

PART 2 | THEOPHILUS' DOCTRINE OF SCRIPTURE

in which the first Christians wrote. The earliest writings of the second century, the Apostolic Fathers, typically represent a practical, devotional, and ecclesial context. The later writings are generally engaged in controversy, either with heretics or with pagans. Therefore, their use of Scripture typically falls short of formal exegesis or commentary.[2] The first formal Christian commentaries that we have do not come until the early third century from Hippolytus and Origen.[3] However, this does not mean that Scripture did not have an important role in this period.

The devotional and pastoral works are filled with Scripture citations and allusions that serve to establish moral practices or doctrines. The *Epistle to the Philippians* by Polycarp is a wonderful example of how allusions to Scripture are so important in these writings.[4] This work seems to be almost an anthology of allusions to passages from the Pauline epistles adapted for Polycarp's context. It is obvious why Scriptures would play such a key role in the anti-heretical works of Irenaeus[5] and Tertullian, but it might be surprising to some to see the key role of Scripture in the apologetic writings engaging with pagan cultures. The Greek Apologists in general, and Theophilus in particular, based their presentation of the superiority of Christianity on the Scriptures.[6] The presentation of the superior Christian philosophy was not independent of but rather guided by and dependent on Scripture.

These three sets of writings from the second century: the Apostolic Fathers, the anti-heretical works, and the Greek Apologists, do not provide us enough evidence to affirm the existence of a formalized canon list in this period. However, we see the authoritative function of the canonical

---

2. Graves, *The Inspiration and Interpretation of Scripture*, 12–3.

3. As seen in the quote by Jerome about Theophilus, it is possible that he had written commentaries on Proverbs and the Gospels, but the statement of Jerome casts some doubt on their genuineness, and, whether they were written by him or not, they are not extant to us. In fact, AA book 2 is primarily made up of biblical commentary on the Genesis narrative.

4. Hartog, *Polycarp and the New Testament*. Cf. Holmes, "Review of *Polycarp and the New Testament*," 781–3.

5. Cf. Grant, *Irenaeus of Lyons*, 29–40; Lawson, *The Biblical Theology of Saint Irenaeus*: "It is clear that S. Irenaeus loves to regard himself as *homo unius libri* [a man of one book]. With him it is fundamental that the Scriptures provide complete proof for all Christian doctrine. . . . They are an independent authority, an authority that speaks for itself. A witness to this is the constant habit of quoting biblical texts in final settlement of matters of all kinds. Irenaeus plainly believes himself to be founding everything upon 'the Book of God'" (23).

6. Kruger, *Christianity at the Crossroads*, 226.

books in how the Apostolic Fathers cited or alluded to Scriptures in order to guide the churches' faith and practice, in how the anti-heretical writers used Scripture to defend sound doctrine and the rule of faith from heresy and false doctrine, and in how the apologists, like Theophilus, used Scripture to defend the Christian system of thought as the only consistent and true religion.

Though the culture was widely illiterate, the early church still valued its texts, and they occupied an important functional role in the life of the churches. These texts were made available to the illiterate Christian through public Scripture reading and catechetical instruction.[7] In this sense, the New Testament canon, though having an important functional role in the second-century church, had not been formally recognized by the church. As Charles Hill and Michael Kruger have pointed out, there was a certain core set of New Testament books that were widely recognized: the four Gospels, Acts, thirteen or fourteen Pauline epistles (with some debate on Hebrews), Revelation, First John, and First Peter.[8] However, though there were still some debate over the exact boundaries of the New Testament canon in this period, which would even continue for another century or so, there was a great consensus on a core canon.

Therefore, it is important to recognize that in the second century the limits of the New Testament canon, and to some degree the Old (due to the influence of the Septuagint[9] and non-canonical works),[10] were in flux. The

---

7. Kruger, *Christianity at the Crossroads*, 169–174.

8. Hill, "'The Truth above All Demonstration': Scripture in the Patristic Period to Augustine," 66; Kruger, *Canon Revisited*, 232: "This is not to say, of course, that by this point the *boundaries* of the emerging canon had solidified. Even though there was an established core, the edges of the canon were still 'fuzzy,' and there were ongoing discussions over a handful of books like Second Peter, Second and Third John, and Revelation." Kruger confessedly leaves out an analysis of the contributions to the canon development made by Theophilus, but he does consider him briefly in *Christianity at the Crossroads*, 213–214.

9. Law, *When God Spoke Greek*.

10. It was actually a contemporary of Theophilus, Melito of Sardis, who provides one of the first Christian lists of the contents of the Old Testament; Eusebius, *Ecclesiastical History*, 4.26.13–4. Roger Beckwith, though recognizing a firming of the Old Testament canon in the second century B.C., says the following with respect to Christians in the second and third century: "The biblical manuscripts in which we find these [Apocryphal] books are of Christian origin, and they probably got into these progressively after AD 200, when Christians (still without their Bible between two covers) were in some cases becoming a bit vague about the distinction between the Old Testament books and other edifying Jewish books which they read." Beckwith, "Intertestamental Judaism, Its

idea of canon itself, though not found explicitly from Antiochene sources at the time of Theophilus, is however found elsewhere in Christendom at the same time of his writing. One key example is the Muratorian Canon, which gives a New Testament canon list that demonstrates a desire to limit the books that were seen as authoritative in the Western part of the empire.[11] Moreover, shortly after Theophilus' time, there is evidence of canonical consciousness in the second bishop that served in Antioch after Theophilus, Serapion, who rejected the *Gospel of Peter* due to its pseudepigraphal and non-apostolic nature. He even presents this idea as something that he received from his predecessors, maybe even Theophilus, though ultimately his appeal is to the apostles themselves.[12]

Likewise, the second-century Christians did have a clear understanding of the canonical and authoritative role of the Old Testament.[13] The Muratorian Canon, for example, refers to the number of the prophets "that is complete." The Christians always had a canon, even when the borders of the New Testament were still "fuzzy." As F. F. Bruce has affirmed,

> It may be thought curious that, when the Christian Church broke loose from Judaism, she did not at the same time break loose from the Jewish scriptures, the Old Testament. But the fact is, that the Christian Church did not consider the Old Testament to be distinctively Jewish literature. She regarded herself, rather than the Jewish people, as the true heir of the law and the prophets. For, as

---

Literature and Its Significance," 79.

11. Kruger, *Canon Revisited*, 230–231. This dating is not a consensus among scholars, though a second-century date is generally accepted. Sundberg seeks to place the idea of canon in the fourth century, which thus affects his dating of the Muratorian canon list. His understanding of canon requires church consensus and an exclusive definition. However, it is important to keep in mind that the canon also has an ontological characteristic in which God determines the contents of the canon, and in between its original writing and the great consensus of the fourth century, the canon already had a functional role beginning even in the first and second century. Sundberg, "The Making of the New Testament Canon," 1216–24; Sundberg, "Canon Muratori: A Fourth-Century List," 1–41; Hahneman, *The Muratorian Fragment and the Development of the Canon*.

12. Eusebius, *Ecclesiastical History*, 6.12.1.

13. M. F. Wiles, "Origen as Biblical Scholar" in *The Cambridge History of the Bible*, eds. P.R. Ackroyd and C.F. Evans, 454–88. "There was never a time when the Church was without written scriptures. From the beginning she had the Old Testament and it was for her the oracles of God" (454). Cf, Paul D. Wegner, Terry L. Wilder, and Darrell L. Bock, "Do We Have the Right Canon?" in *In Defense of the Bible*, eds. Steven B. Cowan and Terry L. Wilder, 395.

the Church believed, Christ was the one in whom both law and prophets found their proper fulfilment.[14]

The understanding of the canonical authority of the Old Testament in the early church is often overlooked in considerations of the canonical consciousness of this period. However, the second-century Christians viewed the Old Testament as the authoritative Word of God and they also saw a collection of New Testament writings that had apostolic authority, though, as has been stated, there was some variation on the barriers of that collection depending on the region.[15] Theophilus' understanding of the canon must be understood in this broader context.

THEOPHILUS' CANON

Theophilus had a very high opinion of the Old Testament Scriptures and was even converted through reading them.[16] He also has subtle hints at the three-fold division of the Law that is found in Philo, Luke 24:44–45, and the preface of *Ecclesiasticus*.[17] Likewise, his chronological argument for the antiquity of Christianity provides some evidence for an Old Testament canon that began with Genesis[18] and ended with Chronicles.[19] However, there also appears to be some conceptual parallels with the *Wisdom of Solomon,* and

---

14. Bruce, *The Spreading Flame,* 221. Cf. also, Preus, "The View of the Bible Held by the Church," 359: "Only after the time of the apologists were the New Testament writings accepted along with the Old Testament. This shift took place as a result of the gradual acceptance of the New Testament canon. The New Testament was therefore considered completely authoritative along with the Old, and the two were now seen as one unit. The New Testament was regarded as the divinely authoritative commentary on the Old."

15. Two clear examples of this are the books of Hebrews and Revelation. Revelation was typically well received in the West while it was at times rejected in the East. On the other hand, Hebrews was often received in the East, but at times rejected in the West. In the rejection of these books there were various considerations that were more important in each region, such as: thoughts concerning authorship, use by groups considered heretical, style, and interpretive and theological difficulties.

16. Grant, *Theophilus of Antioch,* I.14.

17. Beckwith, *Old Testament Canon of the New Testament Church,* 110–66. Cf. Grant, "Bible of Theophilus," 177–8.

18. His canon appears to have begun with Genesis because when he speaks of the story of creation, he says, "These are the first teachings which the divine scripture gives." Grant, *Theophilus of Antioch,* II.10.

19. See chapter 9 of this book. Cf. Beckwith, *Old Testament Canon of the New Testament Church,* 115, 123; Dempster, "'An Extraordinary Fact:' Part 2," 210–4.

possible allusions to *Baruch* and *Maccabees*.[20] He does not make any specific claims about the authority of these books or their relationship with the primary Old Testament canon.

With respect to the New Testament canon, he sees that they are consistent with the Old Testament and inspired by the same Spirit. He refers to the Gospels, even citing John by name,[21] though he is silent on Mark. He uses the Codex Bezae version of Acts in AA II.34.[22] This manuscript version of Acts includes a negative version of the Golden Rule in the apostolic letter in Acts 15:20, 29 that is also used in AA.[23] He also knew of Paul's epistles and referred to them as the "divine word" (ὁ θεῖος λόγος; *ho theios logos*).[24] He refers to almost all of Paul's letters, including the Pastorals (though he does not mention 2 Thessalonians); he probably also knew Hebrews, though he makes no comment that would indicate a belief in Pauline authorship.[25] He also seems to be familiar with First Peter, along with some possible echoes of Second Peter which are not conclusive. He makes a possible reference to Revelation 12:9 in AA II.28, but his knowledge and use of this book in his other writings is confirmed by Eusebius.[26]

Grant summarizes the state of the canon in Theophilus in these words:

> We may conclude, then, that in Theophilus' day the New Testament at Antioch consisted of at least three of the four gospels, the Acts of the Apostles, at least eight Pauline epistles [though expanded to include others in his later writings], possibly the epistles of Peter,

---

20. See chapter 9 of this book.

21. Grant says, "It is the first explicit quotation from John in the history of Christianity;" Grant, "Bible of Theophilus," 186.

22. Grant, "Bible of Theophilus," 188.

23. The Bezae (D) manuscript adds the phrase: "και οσα μη θελουσιν εαυτοις γεινεσθαι ετεροις μη ποιειτε" (*kai osa mē thelousin eautois geinesthai eterois mē poieite*) 'and whatever they do not want to be done to themselves, do not do unto others.'

24. In Grant, "Bible of Theophilus" (1947), 188–189 he indicates that maybe the Pauline epistles were not on equal footing with the Old Testament though on their way to that status; however, in *Greek Apologists* (1988), 164, he says, "The Pauline epistles, including the pastorals, are part of his Bible."

25. The lack of clear references to some of Paul's epistles does not necessarily mean he had a limited Pauline corpus, but rather they were simply not used. The Pauline letters were shared in codex form from early on; there is even some evidence in the first century (2 Pet 3:15–16). Cf. Kruger, *Canon Revisited*, 242–6; Royse, "The Early Text of Paul (and Hebrews)" in *The Early Text of the New Testament*, eds. Charles E. Hill and Michael J. Kruger, 175–203.

26. Eusebius, *Ecclesiastical History*, 4.24.1.

and the Apocalypse. All these works were regarded as inspired, and for the purposes of his apology Theophilus was able to present them as the equivalent of the "writings" of the Jews.[27]

Therefore, it appears that Theophilus was in line with other second-century writings in his use of the 'core' New Testament books in the midst of the church's development of firm canonical boundary lines.[28] The argument of this book does not depend on Theophilus having a complete Old Testament and New Testament canon consisting of only the 66 books of the Protestant Bible. Rather, this book seeks to show that Theophilus understood certain writings called Scripture to be unique and distinct from other literature and to consider what he believed about their nature. For this reason, the main point is not what books he included in this set-apart category, but what is their nature.

THEOPHILUS' USE OF SCRIPTURE

There are three basic ways in which Theophilus incorporates Scripture into his work: (1) extended citations, (2) rhetorical citations, (3) and allusions.[29] Book 2 contains several extended citations from the book of Genesis which are then followed by exegesis. In books 1 and 3, the quotes and allusions are weaved into the discourse in a more rhetorical fashion. As Grant points out, "In I.3 and III.15 his use of Scripture is allusive rather than explicit. But the purpose is the same; it is to create scripturally-grounded theological statements."[30] In another place he says, "He is the first Christian writer to reproduce pages of the Old Testament; he quotes extensively from the New Testament; and his theological outlook is based on the Bible."[31] Also, in line with the thesis of this book, Parsons says, "Scripture played a central, fairly unique, and essential role in this truly brilliantly-conceived structure.

---

27. Grant, "Bible of Theophilus," 188.

28. The only apparent exception to this is the apparent lack of any clear reference to First John, but to deny that it was part of his canon would be an argument from silence; and, due to us only having one rather small work of his extant, it is a rather loud silence.

29. Parsons, *Ancient Apologetic Exegesis*, deals primarily with the sources that Theophilus used for his use of Scripture. He examines his use of copying from biblical manuscripts, the use of memory from extensive Scripture study, and also the possible use of testimonia sources.

30. Grant, "Scripture, Rhetoric, and Theology," 33.

31. Grant, "Bible of Theophilus," 173.

Part 2 | Theophilus' Doctrine of Scripture

If we miss the ancient rhetorical role of Scripture in *Ad Autolycum*, we misunderstand Theophilus himself."[32]

Since the late 1800s, there have been attempts at cataloging the citations and allusions of Scripture in AA. For example, Otto identified some allusions that were based on weak lexical correspondence, and better lists have been produced by Grant and others.[33] The power of an allusion is important for understanding Theophilus, as well as many other Christian writers.[34] An allusion is an intentional though implicit and partial reproduction of a text. Though Theophilus often uses Old Testament *citations* in defense of his arguments,[35] many times, especially with respect to Christian virtue[36] and his teaching on the Logos, he undergirds them with various and powerful New Testament allusions.[37]

There are 52 citations in the three books of Autolycus (44 from Old Testament and 8 from New Testament).[38] Several of these citations are extended citations that are used as a basis for extended exegesis and theological development: specifically the citations in Book 2 of Genesis 1:3–2:3,[39] 2:4–7,[40] 2:8–3:19,[41] 4:9–14,[42] and 4:17–22[43]. Parsons identifies a total (citations and allusions) of 279 scriptural references in AA: 45 in book 1, 105 in book 2, and 129 in book 3. Out of the 21,602 words in the three

---

32. Parsons, *Ancient Apologetic Exegesis*, ch. 1.

33. Otto, "Gebrauch neutestamentlicher Schriften bei Theophilus von Antiochien."

34. Parsons affirms, "When a passage is merely alluded to, rather than explicitly cited, the reader is forced to engage in the process of locating the parallel in Scripture. I believe that this requirement for reader engagement endows allusions with greater literary power than citations. Readers are forced to become engaged intellectually to a greater degree;" Parsons, "By One and the Same Spirit," 17.

35. As will be seen later, this is likely due to the fact that one of his goals is to prove the antiquity of Christianity and its writings.

36. Grant, *Theophilus of Antioch*, III.15.

37. Grant, "Scripture, Rhetoric, and Theology," 38. Here Grant shows how his understanding of Logos is informed by allusions to Luke 1:35 and John 1:14: "That is to say that underneath Theophilus' expressions lies the New Testament."

38. For a full list of citations and allusions in Theophilus see Appendix 1. In contrast with the argument of Allert, freedom in citation was due to the nature of rhetoric and allusion and not a sign of lesser authority. Cf. Hill, "Truth above All Demonstration," 73.

39. Grant, *Theophilus of Antioch*, II.11.

40. Grant, *Theophilus of Antioch*, II.19

41. Grant, *Theophilus of Antioch*, II.20–1

42. Grant, *Theophilus of Antioch*, II.29.

43. Grant, *Theophilus of Antioch*, II.30.

books, he identifies 4,567 (284 in book 1, 3,096 in book 2, 1,188 in book 3) as being from Scripture. With this data, 21.1 percent of AA comes directly from Scripture either through citation or allusion.[44]

This brief survey of his understanding of the limits of Scripture (as far as one can tell from his only remaining work) and his use of Scripture provides a helpful and necessary introduction to understanding his doctrine of Scripture, as addressed in the following chapters.

---

44. Parsons, *Ancient Apologetic Exegesis*, Appendix 2.

5

"The Light of the Sun"

Theophilus' Doctrine of the Necessity of Revelation

THEOPHILUS, LIKE OTHER CHURCH fathers of the second century, certainly had a high view of Scripture, what is here called his *doctrine of Scripture*. For Theophilus, Scripture is the very warp and woof of his worldview and his presentation of the superiority of Christianity. The Scriptures are the authoritative witness for what Christianity believes about God, the world, and ethics. This section of the book will systematize Theophilus' view of Scripture by analyzing three main sources of evidence: (1) his explicit affirmations about the nature of Scripture, including their necessity, authority, inspiration, antiquity, and consistency; (2) the placement of these affirmations about Scripture in his overall rhetorical structure, (3) and the subtle yet key role that Scripture allusions and citations have in the rhetorical structure of his work.

Before analyzing his affirmations about Scripture and his use of Scripture, it is important to make a few disclaimers about the nature and limitations of this endeavor. First, just as Scripture itself does not formally present a systematic doctrine of Scripture as one would expect from a systematic theology, neither does Theophilus; however, they both give us key affirmations that can serve as the necessary pieces for developing such a systematic presentation of the doctrine of Scripture.[1] Therefore, we will discuss sev-

---

1. It must be clarified that in the opinion of the present author, what Scripture has to say about itself is not merely descriptive of what its human authors thought about Scripture; it is much more than that. What Scripture has to say about itself is prescriptive

eral of Theophilus' key teachings about the nature of divine revelation and Scripture specifically and we will try to see the way they interact together in his apology.

Determining the doctrine of Scripture according to the church fathers of the second century and even into the early third is a difficult task.[2] Some have even said that such a task is inappropriate given the early stage in which these writers found themselves in the development of the canon into what the church has today.[3] As Charles Hill points out,

> The general dearth of lengthy systematic reflection on the doctrine of Scripture in this period [the early church], and the historical delay and disorder in achieving a consensus on the canon, have convinced some that a high respect for Scripture and a conviction of its central importance for the life of the church is a Protestant thing, or more narrowly, a product of Protestant evangelicalism and therefore very much a historically circumscribed phenomenon. In the patristic period, it is thought, there was no canon of Scripture to appeal to, only a canon or rule of faith. And while the Scriptures, particularly the Jewish Scriptures, were regarded as authoritative, they were not consulted as much as were the various creedal summaries and an authoritative church hierarchy. The growing influence of specifically Christian writings (later called the New Testament) is often depicted as gradual, as is the slow dawn of the idea that there ought to be a limit to the number of books to which authoritative appeal in the church should be made.[4]

---

for the Christian; that is, what Scripture says about itself is authoritative and demands our belief. However, what Theophilus says about Scripture does not have such authority, as he himself would affirm, but we hope to see how Theophilus not only understands the Scriptures in accordance with Scripture, but also in accordance with many others in his day. Also, the affirmations of the Scriptures give us much greater evidence with which to develop a complete doctrine of Scripture.

2. As Keith Mathison also affirms, "Among the apostolic fathers, one will search in vain to discover a formally outlined doctrine of Scripture such as may be found in modern systematic theology textbooks;" Mathison, *The Shape of Sola Scriptura*, 20.

3. This flows from a desire to remove theological considerations from an analysis of the history of the canon's development. However, as Kruger and others have pointed out, the canon is a theological idea, and thus a consideration of a church father's *ontology* of Scripture is helpful and necessary for understanding his contribution to the canon's development. Kruger, "The Definition of 'Canon.'"

4. Hill, "'The Truth above All Demonstration,'" 43–4. This article provides a systematic presentation of the doctrine of Scripture in the early church similar to this book. However, his scope is much broader and many of his sources come from the third and fourth century.

Part 2 | Theophilus' Doctrine of Scripture

Though it is true that there is no formal development of a doctrine of Scripture in this period,[5] it appears clear that the fathers of this period believed and affirmed key tenets regarding the nature of the books that feature so prominently in their writing. Though they do not give us the fully-developed doctrinal affirmations of later generations, this does not mean that they did not express their own thoughts on the nature of Scripture.

Second, due to the limited access that we have to Theophilus' thought, this book does not seek to present everything that he thought about Scripture; this would claim too much. Though it is limited to his affirmations in AA, it does seek thoroughness in its presentation of the doctrine of Scripture according to AA.[6] However, it is safe to say that his teachings on Scripture in this book are characteristic of his thought in general due to the foundational role that they play in his worldview system.[7]

This is an important observation that has not been fully appreciated in some scholarship on Theophilus. For example, Bentivegna and Grant have both rightly pointed out that Jesus Christ is not mentioned explicitly in AA, however, this has led them to make generalizations about his whole theological system by saying that he did not see Christ or his work as central to Christian theology, or at best he had an adoptionist view of Christ.[8] The fact is that there is not sufficient evidence to make such claims. Therefore, I prefer to follow Parsons example of an "agnostic" approach to Theophilus' Christology, and thus explain such lacks in light of the rhetorical and protreptic nature of AA.[9] On the other hand, his view of Scripture does play a central role in his argument in AA and is the basis on which he defends his presentation of the Christian worldview. Therefore, it seems more appropriate to argue that since Scripture plays such a key role in defending

---

5. Origen's *De principiis* 4.1 is often considered the first attempt at such a systematic presentation of the nature of Scripture. This work can be dated to around the first quarter of the third century. Therefore, there is no formal, systematic presentation of the doctrine of Scripture in the second century.

6. For example, a common teaching about the nature of Scripture that is found in second-century writers is how all of Scripture centers around Christ. This affirmation does not appear in Theophilus, and we do not have enough evidence to affirm that it was or wasn't a part of his thought.

7. Other doctrines that he develops more clearly, clear enough for firm assertions, are his view of the "monarchy" of God and creation *ex nihilo*, along with providence, ethics, resurrection, and eternal judgement. See ch. 3 of the present work for an introduction to his beliefs on these teachings.

8. Benitvegna, "Christianity without Christ;" Grant, *Jesus after the Gospels*, 77–8

9. Parsons, *Ancient Apologetic Exegesis*.

and presenting the foundational principles of his faith in AA it would have played a key role in other areas of his thinking as well. On the other hand, it is an argument from silence (especially in light of the small portion of his writings that are extant) to argue that since Christ does not have a central role in AA, he must not have been central to his thinking in other areas. Therefore, this book seeks to avoid this danger by focusing on what can confidently be deduced about his view of Scripture from his affirmations about Scripture and the way he uses them in his defense of Christianity.

Third, we will analyze first and primarily the doctrine of Scripture in Theophilus himself, and then we will briefly compare his affirmations with those of other second-century church fathers. This corroborating evidence from his contemporaries does not represent an exhaustive discussion of their understanding of Scripture. Rather, this evidence will show that Theophilus was not alone in his high view of Scripture, and it may be a stimulus for others to provide thorough analyses of these church fathers and their understanding of canon, scriptural authority, and inspiration.

One last disclaimer must be made due to the non-systematic way in which Theophilus presents his understanding of Scripture along with the intimate connection that there is naturally between the authority, inspiration, consistency, and antiquity of Scripture. For these two reasons, the quotes and headings of this section cannot be dedicated exclusively to its respective topic. There will be some overlap. However, this will foster a greater appreciation for the rhetorical role that Scripture plays in his work, and the foundational authority that they have in his faith. Also, this reality ensures that the connections made in this book truly come from Theophilus and not from a preconceived system imposed on him by the current author.

THE NECESSITY OF REVELATION

The first attribute of divine revelation that Theophilus addresses in his apology, which also makes a fitting start for a systematic treatment of revelation and Scripture, is the necessity of divine revelation. Though this first attribute addresses more broadly the nature of divine revelation, which also appears in creation and providence, he states that it is the same Logos and Sophia that reveals the Father in creation and providence that also revealed him and his holy law to the holy prophets. Across his work, he develops three main reasons why revelation is necessary: (1) revelation is necessary to know God, (2) revelation is necessary because God made man dependent upon his light, (3) revelation is necessary for the preservation of the world from disorder and chaos.

Revelation and the Knowledge of God

The first argument to which Theophilus responds is a request from Autolycus for Theophilus to show him his God. In his response to this request, Theophilus identifies two main problems that restrict man from seeing or comprehending God—man's sin and God's transcendence. The solution to these problems is the light of divine revelation.

First, because of man's sinful state, man cannot rightly understand God's revelation. Theophilus affirms that sinful man is unable to see and understand God unless God makes him able:

> For God is seen by those who are capable of seeing Him, once they have the eyes of the soul opened. All have eyes, but some have eyes which are hooded and do not see the light of the sun. Just because the blind do not see, however, the light of the sun does not fail to shine; the blind must blame themselves and their eyes. So you also, O man, hast cataracts over the eyes of your soul overspread because of your sins and wicked deeds. Just as a man must keep a mirror polished, so he must keep his soul pure. When there is rust on a mirror, a man's face cannot be seen in it; so also when there is sin in a man, such a man cannot see God.[10]

In this passage Theophilus says that God is only made known to those who repent and wash themselves of their sin. It is sin that has blinded the eyes of man from seeing and understanding God. For this reason, it requires a work of God's mercy for man to know him and believe. He concludes I.2 with these words, "All this [your immorality] brings darkness upon you, just as when a flux of matter comes over the eyes and they cannot see the light of the sun. So also, O man, your ungodliness brings darkness upon you and you cannot see God."[11]

Just because man is blind does not mean that God has not revealed himself. Though God reveals himself plainly in nature[12] and has also revealed himself in Scripture,[13] it requires God's grace and man's repentance

---

10. Grant, *Theophilus of Antioch*, I.2.
11. Grant, *Theophilus of Antioch*, I.2.
12. Grant, *Theophilus of Antioch*, I.5–6.
13. Grant, *Theophilus of Antioch*, I.14.

"The Light of the Sun"

for man to truly see. Sin is the reason for man's blindness. Therefore, God must wash a man's eyes and remove the cataracts from the eyes of his soul so that he can truly see God.

After describing the various ways in which creation demonstrates the glory of God,[14] he then gives a call for Autolycus to go to the divine Physician who alone can cure his blindness:

> You speak of him, O man; you breathe his breath; [yet] you do not know him. This has happened to you because of the blindness of your soul and your heart, but if you will you can be cured. Deliver yourself to the physician, and he will couch the eyes of your soul and heart. Who is the physician? He is God, who heals and gives life through Logos and Sophia.[15]

This is actually the same truth with which Theophilus ends his discourse. It is because man prefers vanities and goes on in his sin that they "have not found the truth."[16] But, when man turns to the Scriptures and submits to the truth God has revealed in faith,[17] there he finds life, righteousness, and truth. Faith is the means by which the eyes are opened, and faith and the fear of the Lord (Prov 1:7) are necessary for any understanding or sight of God.[18]

Secondly, because of God's infinitude and incomprehensibility,[19] man cannot approach unto him without God first making himself known to him. He is not like the foolish, pagan idols that can be contained, comprehended, and need to be carried around by men. For Theophilus, finite man cannot contain or comprehend the infinite God. He demonstrates this point by three analogies: that of the sun, a pomegranate, and an unseen king.

> If a man cannot stare at the sun, though it is a very small star, because of its overwhelming heat and power, how much more is it the case that a mortal man cannot view the glory of God which is inexpressible! As a pomegranate, with a rind surrounding it, has inside many cells and cases, separated by membranes, and has many seeds dwelling in it, so the whole creation is surround by the spirit of God and the surrounding spirit, along with the creation,

---

14. Grant, *Theophilus of Antioch*, I.5–7.
15. Grant, *Theophilus of Antioch*, I.7.
16. Grant, *Theophilus of Antioch*, III.30.
17. Grant, *Theophilus of Antioch*, I.14.
18. Grant, *Theophilus of Antioch*, I.8.
19. Grant, *Theophilus of Antioch*, I.3–4.

is enclosed by the hand of God. As the pomegranate seed, dwelling inside, cannot see what is outside the rind since it is itself inside, so man, who with the whole creation is enclosed by the hand of God, cannot see God.

A king on earth is believed to exist even if he is not seen by all; he is apprehended by means of his laws and commands and authorities and powers and images. Are you unwilling to apprehend God through his works and powers?[20]

These illustrations serve to show the foolishness of Autolycus's search for a God that can be seen, touched, and handled. Theophilus proves through these illustrations and various scriptural references, that God is above creation—transcendent—, but he at the same time condescends to provide a remedy for man's spiritual blindness[21] and to patiently teach man the truth and the way of righteousness. This balance between the (1) incomprehensibility and transcendence of God and (2) the knowability and immanence of God can be seen clearly in I.3:

[1] Hear me, O man: the form of God is ineffable and inexpressible, since it cannot be seen with merely human eyes [unlike the idols]. For he is in glory uncontainable, in greatness incomprehensible, in loftiness inconceivable, in strength incomparable, in wisdom unteachable, in goodness inimitable, in beneficence inexpressible....
[2] You will say to me, then: 'Is God angry?' Certainly: he is angry with those who do evil deeds, but good and kind and merciful toward those who love and fear him. He is the instructor of the godly and the father of the righteous, but the judge and punisher of the ungodly.[22]

Because of the realities of man's sin and God's transcendence, he who wants to know God must first submit to him in faith and fear. God must open man's blind eyes and gently teach him the truth if he would have any hope of truly knowing the one and only God.

Theophilus sees Scripture and the internal work of the Logos and Sophia as the way in which God resolves both of these problems.[23] However, the full solution to this problem is experienced at the resurrection. As he

20. Grant, *Theophilus of Antioch*, I.5.

21. Grant, *Theophilus of Antioch*, I.7.

22. Grant, *Theophilus of Antioch*, I.3. Similar affirmations are often found in Christian reflection on the question of how man can know God; cf. Calvin, *Institutes of the Christian Religion*, 1:65; Hodge, *Systematic Theology*, 1:338.

23. Grant, *Theophilus of Antioch*, I.7.

says, "When you put off what is mortal and put on imperishability (cf. 1 Cor. 15:53f.), then you will rightly see God. For God raises up your flesh immortal with your soul; after becoming immortal you will then see the Immortal, if you believe in him now. Then you will know that you unjustly spoke against him."[24] The only sure way of getting to a fuller experience of the knowledge of God later, in the resurrection, is by submitting to him in faith now.

Revelation and God's Design in Creation

Theophilus also presents the necessity of revelation in his commentary on the Hexameron, "the six days of creation."[25] In II.15, he makes the earliest explicit mention of the Trinity, even earlier than Tertullian by at least a decade.[26] He gives a moral allegorical interpretation of the days of creation and says that the first three days all relate to one of the three persons of the "Trinity [τριάς; trias]"—"God, and his Logos, and his Sophia." The fourth day is compared to man, who he says "is in need of light."[27] On the fourth day, God made the luminaries because man is dependent upon God for light; that is, man is dependent upon God's revelation. Those who obey "the law and the commandments of God" are compared to those stars who keep their ordained course. But those that move like the planets are compared to those who abandon "His law and ordinances."[28] He uses this allegorical interpretation to affirm that since God has created man, man is therefore dependent upon God and his revelation.

Revelation and the World's Preservation

In another passage where Theophilus shows the necessity of revelation, he claims that without God's revelation, specifically his revelation in the Scriptures, the world would have been consumed by chaos:

---

24. Grant, *Theophilus of Antioch*, I.7.
25. According to McVey, Theophilus is the first one to use this term. McVey, "The Use of Stoic Cosmogony in Theophilus of Antioch's *Hexaemeron*," 32–58.
26. For Tertullian's doctrine of the Trinity see Tertullian, *Against Praxeas*, ch. 12 in ANF 3:606–7 and Litfin, "Tertullian on the Trinity," 81–98.
27. Grant, *Theophilus of Antioch*, II.15.
28. Grant, *Theophilus of Antioch*, II.15.

> And we say that for us the world is in the likeness of the sea. For jut as the sea, if it did not have the flow of rivers and springs as a supply of nourishment, would long ago have been parched because of its saltiness; so also the world, if it had not had the law of God and the prophets flowing and gushing forth sweetness and compassion and righteousness, and the teaching of God's holy commandments, would already have failed, because of the evil and sin in it.[29]

Here he makes the claim that just as the rivers continually fill the sea and give balance and nourishment to the sea, even so the Scriptures preserve the world from completely undoing itself. This passage does not refer to the necessity of revelation to know God, rather it says that revelation is necessary for the world to continue as it is without destroying itself. God's Word is the life-giving fountain that preserves and nourishes the world.

For Theophilus, if man were left to his own devices and wisdom, then he would have never been able to discover the truth. The vain attempts of poets and philosophers merely demonstrate the inability of man to discover the truth without God's revelation. However, in God's mercy he did not leave man to his own devices: "The God and Father and Maker of the universe did not abandon mankind but gave a law and sent holy prophets to proclaim and to teach the human race that each one of us might become sober and recognize that God is one."[30] In God's wisdom he revealed the truth through the Spirit to his prophets so that man could know and believe the truth—not only the truth about God and creation, but also how to live a godly life. According to Theophilus, divine revelation was an act of God's grace in which he preserved the world from completely undoing itself by its own sin and error.

Likewise, Theophilus himself often recognizes his dependence on divine help in communicating the truth of the Christian faith, and the necessity of divine intervention for Autolycus's repentance. This heart is communicated in a short prayer that he records in III.23: "I ask favour from the only God that I may speak the whole truth exactly, in accordance with his will, so that you and everyone who reads these books may be led by his truth and grace."[31]

---

29. Grant, *Theophilus of Antioch*, II.14.
30. Grant, *Theophilus of Antioch*, II.34.
31. Grant, *Theophilus of Antioch*, III.23.

Revelation's Necessity and the Second Century

This teaching of the necessity of divine revelation is also seen in other apologists of the second century. In *The Letter to Diognetus*, this is a major teaching that shows up repeatedly. Though the author of this letter is unknown, it is frequently dated around the middle of the second century. The author affirms that the Christian system is not merely the product of human reasoning, but it is the direct result of God's self-disclosure in him who is the Word. As he says, "Certainly, this creed of theirs [the Christians] is no discovery due to some fancy or speculation of inquisitive men; nor do they, as some do, champion a doctrine of human origin."[32]

Later, he alludes to the work of the pre-Socratic philosophers like Heraclitus (fl. ca. 500 BC) and Thales (fl. 580–540 BC) who affirmed that the ultimate essence, or "God," is fire or water.[33] However, he concludes, "No, this is nothing but jugglery and imposture dished up by quacks. 5 No man has either seen or made known God; but He has revealed Himself. 6 And He did reveal Himself by faith, through which alone it has been vouchsafed us to see God."[34] Therefore, like in Theophilus, it is not the reason of man that leads to knowledge, but it is faith in God's revelation that leads to understanding. Likewise, he also emphasizes how the Christian God is the unseen God, unlike the material idols of the pagans, but he is not the "unknown God" of Athens (Acts 17:23), since he has chosen to reveal himself and to be known by all those who have faith.

In analyzing the apologetic principles that are seen in this letter and also in other early church apologies, Michael Haykin says, ". . .men and women are unable to reason their way to the truth without God's help. If God is to be found, he must reveal himself to the seeking heart. The author thus stresses the provision that God has made for finding him through the revelation of himself in his Son, Jesus Christ."[35] Like Theophilus, *The Letter to Diognetus* affirms the absolute necessity of divine revelation, and this revelation is found in Scripture and ultimately in the divine Logos.

---

32. Quasten and Plumpe, eds., *The Didache, The Epistle of Barnabas, The Epistles and the Martyrdom of St. Polycarp, The Fragments of Papias and The Epistle to Diognetus*, 138–139: ch. 5.3.

33. Quasten and Plumpe, eds., *The Letter to Diognetus*, 142: ch. 8.1–3.

34. Quasten and Plumpe, eds., *The Letter to Diognetus*, 142: ch. 8.4–6.

35. Haykin, *Rediscovering the Church Fathers*, 66.

6

"Counsellor and Pledge"

Theophilus' Doctrine of the Authority of Scripture

THE SECOND ATTRIBUTE OF Scripture that is affirmed repeatedly in AA is the authority of Scripture. As we have seen already in his apologetic purpose, Theophilus is seeking to show the superiority of the Christian way of thinking and living, and he bases his arguments on the authoritative divine words of Scripture. He clearly sees Scripture as possessing a higher authority than other writings, including his own. As Grant says, "Moreover elsewhere he does not refer to his own works in this way [as authoritative and definitive on the events of Creation] and he is eager for Autolycus to read the inspired scriptures."[1] The editors of the ANF series say, "[Theophilus] evidently had a profound acquaintance with the inspired writings, and he powerfully exhibits their immense superiority in every respect over the heathen poetry and philosophy."[2] Theophilus displays his understanding of scriptural authority as the only consistent source of truth and ethics through (1) his explicit affirmations, (2) his description of Scripture as holy and divine, and (3) his rhetorical structures.

---

1. Grant, "The Bible of Theophilus," 174. Cf. Grant, *Theophilus of Antioch*, III.1.

2. Alexander Roberts, James Donaldson, and A. Cleveland Coxe, eds., "Introductory Note to Theophilus of Antioch," in ANF 2:88.

EXPLICIT AFFIRMATIONS

One of the first explicit affirmations about the authority of Scripture is found in I.14. He concludes his first book by a short account of his own conversion and a call for Autolycus to believe the Scriptures and to obey God lest he fall under eternal judgment. He first shows how the Scriptures (primarily the Old Testament) were instrumental in his own conversion: "At that time I encountered the sacred writings of the holy prophets, who through the Spirit of God foretold past events in the way that they happened, present events in the way they are happening, and future events in the order in which they will be accomplished."[3] In this affirmation, Theophilus gives the reader a glimpse into the foundational role that Scripture played, not only in his philosophical thought, but also in his very life and identity as a Christian. To use a biblical metaphor, Theophilus saw himself as having been "born again not of perishable seed but of imperishable, through the living and abiding Word of God" (1 Pet 1:23).

The authority of Scripture is essentially the teaching that what Scripture affirms should be believed and what Scripture commands should be obeyed. In other words, Scripture is the rule for a Christian's faith and life. This is precisely what we see in this affirmation. When Scripture talks about past events it is "in the way they happened," when it speaks of ongoing realities it is exactly what we see happening, and when it predicts the future, we can trust that these events will be accomplished in the precise order given in the scriptural word. Theophilus seems to have been convinced by the authority and truthfulness of Scripture in the way that it consistently and rightly speaks the truth about the past, present, and future.[4]

Because of the influence of the Scriptures in his conversion, Rogers says, "He is, however, a man highly committed to 'the sacred writings of the holy prophets'. . . . [H]is theology features the role of these prophets who were the agents of his own transformation from a doubting Theophilus."[5]

---

3. Grant, *Theophilus of Antioch*, I.14.

4. It may be the case that the reader has certain convictions about the historicity and truthfulness of Scripture because of which he would not speak in the same way as Theophilus here. However, this does not provide a basis for disagreeing with the present affirmations because what we are arguing for is what Theophilus thought about Scripture. Though a reader may have his own doubts about Scripture's affirmations about the past, present, or future, the fact is that Theophilus did not share that same skepticism toward Scripture.

5. Rogers, "Theophilus of Antioch," 218.

PART 2 | THEOPHILUS' DOCTRINE OF SCRIPTURE

Theophilus shows how the Scriptures were the power of God unto his salvation. He then later gives another call for Autolycus to believe the Christian Scriptures: "If you will, you too must reverently read the prophetic writings. They will be your best guides for escaping the eternal punishments, and obtaining the eternal benefits of God."[6] In this passage, the Scriptures are the best and only way of obtaining salvation, and not only do they show the way of escape from God's wrath, but they also instruct in obedience by which the Christian will receive the eternal rewards that God gives to his people. Scripture's authority and truthfulness were the determinative factor in his own conversion to Christianity, and they would also serve Autolycus in the same way if he diligently and believingly studied them.

Likewise, Theophilus' final words reveal his understanding of the authority of Scripture as well, "If you will, read these books carefully so that you may have a counsellor (σύμβουλον; *sumboulon* cf. Rom 11:34) and pledge (ἀρραβῶνα; *arrabōna* cf. Eph 1:14) of the truth."[7] The Scriptures, which are the antecedent to "these books" in the context (that is, "these books" do not refer to his own writings), act as both counsellor and guarantee of truth for those who would carefully incline their minds to learn from them.[8] They guide and instruct as a wise counsellor, and they serve as the guarantee that truth will be found by all those who study these divine words with faith, love, and fear. The word "pledge" here is the same word used by Paul in Ephesians 1:14 where he speaks of the Holy Spirit as the guarantee and authorizing seal of a believer's future redemption. In a similar way, for any student or philosopher in search of the truth, Theophilus says that the source of truth that provides a sure guide and counsellor for truth's discovery is Scripture.

DISTINCT APPELLATIONS

The second way in which Theophilus demonstrates his belief in the authority of Scripture is by the terms that he uses to describe them. In reference to

---

6. Grant, *Theophilus of Antioch*, I.14.

7. Arndt et al., *BDAG*, en loc. Cf. Grant, *Theophilus of Antioch*, III.30.

8. The reference to "these books" seems to imply a canonical consciousness in Theophilus. Though it is difficult to discern the exact limits of what books Theophilus would have included, as discussed in chapter 4, it is clear that Theophilus had at least a mental conception of some books that serve as a sure "counsellor" and "pledge" of truth that distinguishes them from other works, especially those composed by pagan philosophers.

a quote from Proverbs 24:21, he says that Scriptures are the "Law of God" (ὁ νόμος ὁ τοῦ θεοῦ; *ho nomos ho tou theou*).[9] In I.14 he refers to Scripture as the "sacred writings of the holy prophets;" "ἱεραῖς γραφαῖς τῶν ἁγίων προφητῶν" (*hierais graphais tōn hagiōn prophētōn*)[10] In II.10 he refers to the "divine scriptures" (ἡ θεία γραφή; *hē theia graphē*), which follows a quote from Genesis 1:1–2, Proverbs 8:27–9 and an allusion to Exodus 20:7. He uses the same word to describe a quote from Genesis 1:26 in II.18. In II.13 he refers to them as "holy Scripture" (ἡ ἁγία γραφή; *hē hagia graphē*), in which he is commenting on Genesis 1 and cites Isaiah 40:22.[11] In III.13 he refers to the "holy word" (ὁ ἅγιος λόγος; *ho hagios logos*), which includes citations from Proverbs and Matthew. In III.14, before referring to citations from Romans 13 and First Timothy 2, he refers to the "divine word" (ὁ θεῖος λόγος; *ho theios logos*). In all of these titles, Theophilus sets forth his belief in the Scriptures as literature that is both set apart ("holy" and "sacred") and divine.[12]

Another important appellation that he gives to Scripture is "the word of truth" (τοῦ λόγου τῆς ἀληθείας; *tou logou tēs alētheias*).[13] Submission to Scripture is the requirement for true doctrine and for avoiding heresy. In II.14, Theophilus gives a little glimpse into his anti-heretical works that are no longer extant when he says, "For they [the heretics] are not guided by *the word of truth*, but just as pirates, when they have filled ships, run them on the places mentioned above [islands of error] in order to destroy them, so it happens that those who stray from the truth are destroyed by error." Therefore, the Scriptures are not only necessary for maintaining the world and preserving the church, but they are also the rule for judging heresy from orthodoxy. For Theophilus, Scriptures are a rule for doctrine and for life. This principle is illustrated throughout by his use of Scripture to prove his arguments or to undergird them, but here it is stated more explicitly.

---

9. Grant, *Theophilus of Antioch*, I.11.

10. Grant, *Theophilus of Antioch*, I.14.

11. Cf. Grant, *Theophilus of Antioch*, II.19, 21, 22, where the same phrase appears in the plural form.

12. Parsons recognizes that Theophilus does not explicitly call the New Testament writings "Scripture" in a technical sense, though they clearly had a functional unity with all that was considered "Scripture" in that technical sense (the Old Testament). Parsons, "By One and the Same Spirit," 252.

13. Grant, *Theophilus of Antioch*, II.14.

PART 2 | THEOPHILUS' DOCTRINE OF SCRIPTURE

RHETORICAL FOUNDATION

Third, it is also important to note his engagement with authoritative Greek and Roman texts[14] and the battle that he conducts between them and the Christian's authoritative text. It is in light of this that Parsons quotes Young saying, "Theophilus is the apologist who makes the second-century pagan/Christian 'battle of literatures' most evident."[15] His belief in the authority of Scripture is foundational to his whole argument. If Theophilus did not have such a concept of the superior authority of Scripture, his whole argument then becomes misleading and confused since he consistently upholds Scripture in its teaching on God, man, creation, righteousness, judgement, resurrection, etc. as superior and authoritative.

AA in many parts is the courtroom trial between two literary witnesses: the writings of the prophets and apostles on the one hand, and the pagan philosophers on the other. In order to engage in this trial, Theophilus must demonstrate and uphold the authority of his textual witness. As Parsons has pointed out, establishing the authority of a positive literary witness is the first of the three defensive arguments that were commonly used in ancient rhetoric.[16] It is Scripture, and Scripture alone, that occupies this role as his foundational literary authority for his presentation of the Christian worldview. As will be seen later, he does at times make use of the affirmations of the Greek Sibyl, but her place in his rhetorical structure serves to highlight how Scripture has the supreme authority, and the Sibyl, along with others, serves a corroborating role.

Book 2, chapters 2–8 devote a great amount of time to the analysis and critique of the philosophers and Greek poets. He critiques them for their falsehoods spoken about the nature of God. He attacks them on their claims in each of the main areas of philosophy: ontology, epistemology, and ethics. Though at times he shows some places where the truth shines through in some of the philosophers,[17] there is a strong antithesis between Greek and Christian literature.[18] With respect to ontology, he highlights

---

14. For the role of these authoritative texts see Verheyden, "'Authoritative Texts' and How to Handle Them" in *Christianity in the Second Century*, 189–91. Cf. Young, "The Rhetorical Schools and Their Influence on Patristic Exegesis," 182–99.

15. Parsons, *Ancient Apologetic Exegesis*, ch. 4; cf. Young, "Greek Apologists," 94.

16. Parsons, "By One and the Same Spirit," 40.

17. Grant, *Theophilus of Antioch*, II.37–8.

18. Grant, "Social Setting of Second-Century Christianity," 26. Grant says that there were two main approaches to the relations between Christians and Pagans represented

their falsehoods with respect to the nature of the gods, and especially their claims about a plurality of gods and the possibility of representing the gods in a material form.[19] However, some philosophers did have an idea of one God, like Plato, but he attacks them because of their affirmation of an eternal creation[20] or a denial of providence.[21]

In the second place, he also attacks them on an epistemological basis. First, they are inconsistent and contradict themselves and one another (consistency) and they contradict reality (coherence) in their affirmations about God. Second, when they spoke things that were true it was like honey mixed with poison or a pearl in a swine's snout—truth in a false system that does not lead to God.[22] Third, Theophilus affirms that some truths that they affirmed were stolen from the Old Testament Scriptures since they were earlier than all the philosophers—"borrowed capital."[23] Fourth, the poets and philosophers produced so many errors because they "spoke . . . not by a pure spirit but by one of error;" for they were "inspired by demons and puffed up by them."[24]

In the third place, he attacks the philosophers on the basis of ethics. The gods themselves of the Greeks provide terrible examples of ethics and morality, and not one philosopher has an ethical system as consistent and worthy of obedience as that found in Scripture.[25]

All of the arguments that he uses to remove the foundation behind Autolycus's worldview are countered by the coherence and consistency of the divine Scriptures. As Haykin says, "A good defense of the Christian

---

in the apologists: "attack, presented by Tatian, *in part by Theophilus*, and a little later by Tertullian; and acceptance or compromise, reflected in Apollinaris of Hierapolis, Melito of Sardis, and Athenagoras, and in part by Minicius Felix." Emphasis added. To the first category I would also add the *Letter to Diognetus*, and to the latter Justin Martyr and Clement of Alexandria. Cf. Grant, *Theophilus of Antioch*, III.2.

19. Grant, *Theophilus of Antioch*, II.2–3.
20. Grant, *Theophilus of Antioch*, II.4–7.
21. Grant, *Theophilus of Antioch*, II.8.
22. Grant, *Theophilus of Antioch*, II.12.
23. Bahnsen, *Presuppositional Apologetics*, 96. Cf. Grant, *Theophilus of Antioch*, II.12. Some scholars may point out that there is pagan literature that predates the Scripture and some proponents of forms of literary criticism may give an even later date to most of the biblical literature that makes it contemporary with or after some of the major Greek writers. However, the purpose of this book is to demonstrate what Theophilus himself thought.
24. Grant, *Theophilus of Antioch*, II.8.
25. Grant, *Theophilus of Antioch*, III.2–8.

faith not only displays the problems with rival worldviews, but also sets forth how Christians view the world."[26] Therefore, he transitions from a critique of paganism and pagan literature to a defense of the Christian worldview from the Christian Scriptures. The transition is found in II.9 where he affirms the divine inspiration of the prophets, their consistency, how all of their prophecies have happened as predicted, and his confidence that they will continue to be fulfilled.

The first point refers to the Christian view of ontology and says, "In the first place, in complete harmony [the prophets] they taught us that he [God] made everything out of the non-existent. For there was nothing co-eval with God."[27] This passage is one of the earliest affirmations of the doctrine of creation *ex nihilo* and is one of the key differences that Theophilus sees between the Christian and pagan worldviews. The best someone can find in the philosophers is inconsistency on this point,[28] but the prophets "in complete harmony" teach creation out of nothing.

However, this affirmation of creation *ex nihilo* raises a possible counter argument. How did these prophets know about things before they happened? Is Theophilus not guilty of the same critique he made of the Greeks—speaking about things of which they do not know?[29] This is where he shifts to the nature of Christian epistemology. He answers by an appeal to the generation of the Logos and Sophia before creation and affirms:

> It was he, Spirit of God and Beginning and Sophia and Power of the Most High, who came down into the prophets and spoke through them about the creation of the world and all the rest. For the prophets did not exist when the world came into existence; there were the Sophia of God which is in him and his holy Logos who is always present with him.[30]

Therefore, the prophets could speak truthfully because the very Logos and Sophia, through which God made the heavens and the earth, are active in the life and ministry of the prophets as well. Unlike the spirit of error in the poets and philosophers, the prophets had a "pure spirit," God's very own

---

26. Haykin, "Sharing the Faith: *The Letter to Diognetus*," in *Rediscovering the Church Fathers*, 49–68.

27. Grant, *Theophilus of Antioch*, II.10; cf. II.13.

28. Grant, *Theophilus of Antioch*, II.3–5.

29. As Parsons pointed out, this was a key argument in the standard, ancient manuals of rhetoric. "One and the Same Spirit," 40–41.

30. Grant, *Theophilus of Antioch*, II.10.

Spirit. Therefore, this divine source is what gives Scripture its veracity, credibility, and authority. This quote also demonstrates the interconnectedness of Theophilus' thought. His ontological understanding of the threeness of the one God is intimately connected with his understanding of Scripture. The God who is revealed in Scripture reveals himself through his prophets by his Sophia and his Logos.

Likewise, in Book 3 he looks at the antithesis between the pagan and Christian ethic. Even though the pagans wrongfully and unjustly claim that the Christians are adulterous and incestuous cannibals whose doctrine has only recently come into the world,[31] it is really the pagans and their gods who teach and condone such practices.[32] However, the scriptural ethic is perfectly consistent and coherent and is found in perfect harmony among all the prophets. In III.9 he summarizes the Christian ethic in terms of the Decalogue.[33] There are three main parts to the Christian ethic: piety, which consists of commandments one and two; beneficence, consisting of commandment five; and justice, consisting of commandments six through ten, which he compares with Exodus 23:6–8.[34] Thus the Scriptures are seen as the only authoritative rule for the Christian's way of life, and its ethic is perfectly consistent and purely righteous.

Another way his rhetorical structure demonstrates the authority of Scripture is found in several key passages where he strings together allusions and citations that undergird his argument in a foundational way and provide what will here be called *Scripture-saturated arguments*.[35] The first example, in I.6–7, provides an intimate web of biblical allusions that Theophilus uses rhetorically to highlight the authority of Scripture. Theophilus finds a helpful connection between the request of Autolycus to see Theophilus' God, and the desire of Job to have a meeting with God (Job 9:11, 23:8–9). For this reason, when he discusses how God has revealed himself in nature in I.5–7, after giving some illustrations of that fact in I.5, he then proceeds to weave an intimate web of biblical allusions that draw out much biblical language in order to inform and establish his argument

---

31. Grant, *Theophilus of Antioch*, III.4, 15.

32. Grant, *Theophilus of Antioch*, III.5–8.

33. Cf. Grant, *Greek Apologists*, 161–2; Grant, "The Decalogue in Early Christianity" 1–17.

34. Grant, *Theophilus of Antioch*, III.9.

35. See Appendix 1 under the heading "Organized by AA Placement" to see where the most concentrated uses of biblical citations and allusions appear.

for God's revelation in nature. As God himself responds to Job by an appeal to his acts in nature, even so Theophilus responds in kind to Autolycus.

I.6–7 contain 24 allusions to Scripture. Two of them come from the New Testament. However, 11 of them come from Job (Job 9:8, 9 (2x), 21:15, 34:14, 37:15, 38:10, 18, 22, 31, 35). The book of Job, and especially God's speech in chapter 38, plays a key role in providing the imagery and structure of this section. Parsons has pointed out that this structure not only relies on the various allusions and citations but is intentionally mimicking the structure of the arguments and illustrations that God gives to Job. For this reason, Parsons says, "Yet we would never have known how extensively *Job* shaped Theophilus' argument if we only examined the mere handful of allusions or brief quotations of *Job* listed in biblical indices for *Ad Autolycum*."[36] Through the allusions to Job Theophilus makes it clear he has that text in mind, but this is bolstered by the fact that the structure of his argument in this section follows the lines of God's own defense to Job. The structure as a whole is a form of structural allusion to Job 38–39. The remaining allusions come from Psalms, Proverbs, Ecclesiastes, Isaiah, Jeremiah, and Genesis. This complex construction of biblical allusions serves to demonstrate how even his argument for the existence of God from nature was based on the teaching of Scripture and on a scriptural example of how to respond to a similar question.[37]

Similar strands of scriptural allusions and citations occur in II.10 and 35 and also in III.11–14. In book 2, chapters 10 and 35, the argument is similar. After critiquing the pagan view of God and creation, he then shows how Scripture provides the basis for the Christian's claims,[38] and then gives an extensive commentary on the creation account, commenting mainly for

---

36. Parsons, "Trading Places: Faithful Job and Doubtful Autolycus in Theophilus's Apology," 197. This structure is based on the use of "μετάληψις [*metalēpsis*] and μίμησις [*mimēsis*]," the first of which is similar to an allusion or an echo, while the second is an intentional mimicking not merely of language, but also of imagery and structure (Parsons, "Trading Places," 192).

37. Parsons, "Capstone Example: A Comprehensive Treatment of the Book of Job in Theophilus's Extant Writings," in *Ancient Apologetic Exegesis*, ch. 3. Cf. Parsons, "Trading Places," 197: "For Autolycus' demand to see God, Theophilus found in Scripture a ready-made answer. This was that answer that both Elihu and the Lord gave to Job's *identical* demand. Theophilus realized that God's answer to faithful Job could also transform a doubtful pagan like Autolycus. While Elihu put Job into the shoes of a doubting mocker for justifying himself but not God, Theophilus put the doubting Autolycus into Job's shoes."

38. Grant, *Theophilus of Antioch*, II.9.

apologetic and anti-heretical purposes. However, this exegesis on Genesis 1–11 is bracketed by these two chapters that use Scripture-saturated arguments to show the authority and consistency of the Christian view of God and creation.

II.10 uses three citations (Prov 8:27–29; Gen 1:1 and 1:2) and nine allusions that speak about how God created the world, out of nothing, through the Logos and Sophia. The structure of his argument here is parallel to II.35, wherein he summarizes the teaching from Genesis 1–11 about God and creation and shows that it is the teaching of all of Scripture. In this chapter he uses 10 Old Testament citations, one Old Testament allusion, and three New Testament allusions to show that "[i]t is obvious how agreeably and harmoniously all the prophets spoke, making their proclamation by one and the same Spirit concerning the sole rule of God and the origin of the world and the making of man."[39]

The effect of this long strand of citations and allusions serves to demonstrate that Scripture is the authoritative source for the Christian worldview that he is defending. It even serves as an invitation for the reader to engage with the scriptural text, as Theophilus later makes explicit to Autolycus.[40] The connection we are making is not merely the product of biased rhetorical analysis for he even makes it explicit in his concluding words to this chapter: "And why should I list the multitude of prophets, since they are many and made countless statements in agreement and harmony? For those who desire to do so can read what was said through them and acquire accurate knowledge of what is true, and not be led astray by speculation and pointless labor."[41] In other words, Scripture is the authoritative source of Christianity's superior message about God and the world. This is seen most clearly in the creation account of Genesis 1 but is also confirmed by the consistent witness of texts throughout Theophilus' Scriptures taken from both Old Testament and New Testament books.

The third example of a Scripture-saturated argument is in III.11–14. This is a longer section than the previous arguments, but it consists of a Scripture-saturated argument in order to demonstrate the scriptural ethical principles of repentance (III.11), justice (III.12), chastity (III.13), and relations with non-Christians (III.14).

---

39. Grant, *Theophilus of Antioch*, II.35.
40. Parsons, *Ancient Apologetic Exegesis*, Epilogue.
41. Grant, *Theophilus of Antioch*, II.35.

Part 2 | Theophilus' Doctrine of Scripture

First, III.11 uses five citations from Isaiah, Jeremiah, and Ezekiel to show how God "always wants the human race to turn away from all its sins."[42] This is coupled with an allusion to Deuteronomy and another to the Gospel of John.[43]

Second, III.12 uses 9 citations from Isaiah, Jeremiah, Hosea, Joel, and Zechariah to show the Scripture's consistent teaching on justice and equity. He begins this string of citations with an appeal to scriptural inspiration and consistency: saying, "Furthermore, concerning the justice of which the law spoke [summarized in the Decalogue], the teaching of the prophets and the Gospels is consistent with it because all the inspired men made utterances by means of the one spirit of God."[44] This demonstrates the interconnectedness of Theophilus' affirmation of scriptural authority, consistency, and inspiration.

Third, III.13 speaks of the importance of chastity in the Christian ethical system, and he uses two quotes from Proverbs (Solomon being seen as a "prophet") and two from Matthew ("the gospel voice") to demonstrate it.

Finally, III.14 concludes this section with two citations from Matthew ("the gospel"), one from Isaiah ("Isaiah, the prophet"), and three from Paul ("the divine word") in order to demonstrate how Christians are to act towards their "enemies," those who persecute them, and the state.

This repetition of Scripture-saturated arguments is important for understanding the rhetorical structure of Theophilus and for establishing his understanding of the authority of Scripture as the basis for the Christian ethic. Since the Christian worldview finds its source in the divine and consistent Scriptures, Christians have a superior ethic than what is found in the philosophers.

To summarize, in I.6–7 he uses a Scripture-saturated argument to show the true way of knowing God, in answer to Autolycus's request to "see his God" (epistemology). In II.10 and 35, he uses a Scripture-saturated argument to prove the singularity of God and his creation *ex nihilo* (ontology). In III.11–14, the Scripture-saturated argument returns to show the superiority and coherence of the Christian view of morality (ethics). All of these arguments serve to show the foundational authority of Scripture

---

42. Grant, *Theophilus of Antioch*, III.11.

43. A similar Scripture-saturated argument for the need for repentance is found in *First Clement* 8.

44. Grant, *Theophilus of Antioch*, III.12.

for Theophilus' Christian worldview and its key role in his apologetic methodology.

SCRIPTURE'S AUTHORITY AND THE SECOND CENTURY

It was a common teaching in the early church to see Scripture as the standard for life, doctrine, and worship. As Hill points out, "Though often lost sight of today, the self-authenticating quality of Scripture was perhaps surprisingly well recognized, especially among some early Greek writers."[45] For example, First Clement often alludes to or cites Scripture with reference to particular ethical commands, and he says, "let us do what is written . . . With this commandment and with these instructions let us strengthen ourselves to walk, being obedient to his saintly words, being humble-minded."[46] Also, and much like Theophilus in II.14, Polycarp in his letter to the Philippians held out faithfulness to the apostolic Word as the only sure means of protection from heresy—a rule for doctrine.[47] Like Clement,[48] Hegesippus also held out the Word as the rule, not only for faith and life, but also for the church. He speaks of his journey to Corinth and to Rome and he commends these churches by saying, "But in the case of every succession [of a new bishop], and in every city, the state of affairs is in accordance with the teaching of the Law and of the Prophets and of the Lord."[49] The Scriptures are to regulate the functioning of the church, and she is to ensure that all is done in accordance with the Word of God.[50]

Tatian's *Oration to the Greeks* also has a beautiful statement in which he affirms Scripture's authority and anticipates the discussion of Theophilus' view of scriptural inspiration, antiquity and consistency. He says,

---

45. Hill, "'The Truth above All Demonstration': Scripture in the Patristic Period to Augustine," 46.

46. Clement of Rome, *First Clement* 13.1, 3; Brannan, tran. *The Apostolic Fathers in English*.

47. Polycarp, *Letter to Philippians*, ch. 7.

48. Clement of Rome, *First Clement*, 40–44.

49. Hegesippus, "Fragments from His Five Books of Commentaries on the Acts of the Church," in ANF 8:764.

50. It is interesting that he puts the Law, the Prophets, and the Lord together. This reference to the Lord is most likely to be understood as a reference to the Gospels and the writings of his Apostles.

Part 2 | Theophilus' Doctrine of Scripture

> And, while I was giving my most earnest attention to the matter, I happened to meet with certain barbaric writings, too old to be compared with the opinions of the Greeks, and too divine to be compared with their errors; and I was led to put faith in these by the unpretending cast of the language, the inartificial character of the writers, the foreknowledge displayed of future events, the excellent quality of the precepts, and the declaration of the government of the universe as centred in one Being. And, my soul being taught of God, I discern that the former class of writings lead to condemnation, but that these put an end to the slavery that is in the world, and rescue us from a multiplicity of rulers and ten thousand tyrants, while they give us, not indeed what we had not before received, but what we had received but were prevented by error from retaining.[51]

Though this is just a small glimpse of Tatian's view of Scripture, which merits its own monograph-length treatment, this text demonstrates various similarities to Theophilus. We have already seen how Theophilus also attributed his conversion to Christianity to his encounter with the superiority of the Christian Scriptures. He embraced these books as the sure guide to truth and "precepts" and far superior to the Greek writings to which he had once dedicated his study. Sadly, he saw that these previous books led to tyranny, condemnation, and slavery, while the Christian Scriptures lead to life and freedom. Also, we see similar affirmations about the antiquity and divine character of Scripture. Also, we see the superiority of Scripture in their teaching of "the government of the universe as centred in one Being," similar to Theophilus' idea of the "monarchy" of God. Finally, this quote also shows a similar teaching about how sin and error are the real impediments to man's reception of the plain truth of God. One must be "taught of God" and turn away from error in order to understand the truth found in Scripture.

Therefore, Theophilus is not the only Christian writer in the second century who holds forth Scripture as the rule for faith (ontology and epistemology) and life (ethics)—being the authoritative witness to the only true and consistent philosophy.

---

51. Tatian, "Address of Tatian to the Greeks," in ANF 2:77, [=ch. 29].

7

"Through One and the Same Spirit"

Theophilus' Doctrine of the Inspiration of Scripture

IN THE PREVIOUS CHAPTERS, we saw various evidences of Theophilus' high view of the authority of Scripture. He sees the Scriptures as necessary for a coherent worldview and a reliable witness to who God is, and he also sees Scripture as authoritative for faith and life. Connected to this idea, he also affirms that Scripture is inspired, ancient, and consistent. This chapter seeks to present Theophilus' doctrine of Scripture on his own terms by analyzing various key affirmations that he makes about the role of the Spirit in the production of the Scripture and the relationship among the various parts of Scripture.

Theophilus affirms plainly that the Scriptures were inspired by the Holy Spirit. Though he falls short of giving a full-orbed theory of the mode and function of inspiration, he plainly and repeatedly affirms his confidence in the activity of the Holy Spirit, or Sophia, in the Scriptures and the prophecies of the prophets. We can summarize his teaching on inspiration in this way: inspiration is that work of the Spirit of God (or at times the Logos) by which God spoke through godly men—prophets and apostles—and thus ensured the divine authority, internal consistency (in doctrine or ethic), and external coherence (in history or metaphysic) of all that they said or wrote.[1]

---

1. Note the similarity between this definition and that given in Warfield, *The Works of Benjamin B. Warfield: Revelation and Inspiration*, 1:77–78. "Inspiration is, therefore,

Some of the Greek philosophers and poets claimed some form of divine inspiration as well. In Ancient Greece, sometimes inspiration was connected to an ecstatic and frenzied vision, sometimes it was a reference to divine guidance in composition, and at other times to divine influence that was mediated through human faults and errors.[2] Theophilus not only sets the inspiration of the "holy prophets" by the pure Spirit of God apart from the works of the philosophers and poets which are not consistent or authoritative, but he even affirms that at times the so-called "inspiration" of the philosopher and poet was not divine but demonic.[3] For this reason, there is some truth to the claim of one writer when he says, "there is room to argue (and others *have* argued it) that Theophilus held *all* (or at least most) writings to have been inspired by *some* higher power, with Christian writings (both scriptural and non-scriptural) being those that were inspired by the Christian God."[4] However, at least with regards to the Greek poets and philosophers the "higher power" that inspired them was a demonic force that was actively leading them into error away from the truth of God that shined before them in Creation and the prophetic Scriptures. Therefore, though Theophilus may apply the language of "inspired" to more than just the Scriptures, he understands scriptural inspiration to be unique.

DISTINCT TERMINOLOGY

Before defending the definition of inspiration according to Theophilus, it is important to first summarize the language that he uses to describe this phenomenon. He uses three different phrases or images to describe

---

usually defined as a supernatural influence exerted on the sacred writers by the Spirit of God, by virtue of which their writings are given Divine trustworthiness."

2. D. Jeffrey Bingham discusses various ideas of inspiration found in Classical and Hellensitic Greek sources in his article on inspiration in Athenagoras. Bingham, "'We Have the Prophets:' Inspiration and the Prophets in Athenagoras of Athens," 211–42.

3. Grant, *Theophilus of Antioch*, II.8, 33. Theophilus' awareness of the Greek idea of inspiration and the contrast he establishes between it and his idea of biblical inspiration can be clearly seen in II.8: "So unwillingly they admit that they do not know the truth. Inspired by demons [ὑπὸ δαιμόνων δὲ ἐμπνευσθέντες; *hupo daimonōn de empneusthentes*] and puffed up by them, they said what they said through them. For such poets as Homer and Hesiod, inspired [ἐμπνευσθέντες; *empneusthentes*] as they say by the Muses, spoke out of imagination and error, not by a pure spirit but by one of error." Note that the language of inspiration applied to the poets is different than that used of the biblical writers. Grant, *Theophilus of Antioch*, II.8.

4. Poirier, "Stuart Parsons: *Ancient Apologetic Exegesis*."

inspiration. First, he uses the compound term "πνευματοφόρος" (*pneumatophoros*) three times: twice with the addition of the name "πνεῦμα ἅγιον" (*pneuma hagion*)[5] and another time by itself.[6] This term probably refers to those who are borne along by the Spirit in their prophesying and/or writing, and it appears to be a compound form of the similar language used in Second Peter 1:21 to describe the Spirit's work in the prophets. The word may be translated as "borne by the Spirit" or as "Spirit-bearing," but either way the emphasis is on the activity of the Holy Spirit in the prophetic and apostolic ministries.

The second way he speaks of inspiration is through the image of mediated speech. Frequently, he uses a speech verb of teaching or speaking and indicates the secondary agent with a preposition. In some places he refers to the Holy Spirit who "taught [διδάσκει; *didaskei*] . . . through [διά; *dia*]" the prophets,[7] and other times it is the Holy Spirit who "speaks in the holy prophets [λαλήσαντος ἐν τοῖς ἁγίοις προφήταις; *lalēsantos en tois hagiois prophētais*]."[8] Interestingly, he also uses the prophets as the subject of the speech verb, and the Spirit as the object of the preposition. For example, in I.14, he says that the prophets "foretold through the Spirit of God [προεῖπον διὰ πνεύματος θεοῦ; *proeipon dia pneumatos theou*]."[9]

Finally, he uses the image of containing or being filled [χωρέω; *chōreō*[10]] when he speaks of the prophets "who were filled with the Holy Spirit of God" [τῶν χωρησάντων τὸ ἅγιον πνεῦμα τοῦ θεοῦ; *tōn chōrēsantōn to hagion pneuma tou theou*].[11]

To summarize, Theophilus speaks of inspiration by referring to the prophets as being "borne by the Spirit," as speaking through the Spirit, or by being filled with the Spirit. The remainder of this chapter will look at his explicit affirmations of inspiration and the key rhetorical role that inspiration plays in his apology.

---

5. Grant, *Theophilus of Antioch*, II.9, III.12.

6. Grant, *Theophilus of Antioch*, II.22.

7. Grant, *Theophilus of Antioch*, II.30.

8. Grant, *Theophilus of Antioch*, II.33. In this example, the verb διδάσκω (*didaskō*) is used to refer to how the Holy Spirit teaches every Christian [οἵτινες ὑπὸ πνεύματος ἁγίου διδασκόμεθα; *hoitines hupo pneumatos hagiou didaskometha*] cf. II.30, but the Spirit's work in the prophets here is distinguished by the use of λαλέω (*laleō*).

9. Grant, *Theophilus of Antioch*, I.14.

10. Arndt et al., *BDAG*, en loc.

11. Grant, *Theophilus of Antioch*, III.17.

Part 2 | Theophilus' Doctrine of Scripture

EXPLICIT AFFIRMATIONS

One of his clearest affirmations of scriptural inspiration is in the second book: "The men of God, who were possessed by a holy Spirit [or being borne along by the Holy Spirit; πνευματοφόροι πνεύματος ἁγίου; *pneumatophoroi pneumatos hagiou*] and became prophets and were inspired and instructed by God himself, were taught by God, and became holy and righteous."[12] According to Theophilus, the inspiration of the Holy Spirit was essential to the nature of a prophet.[13] And this inspiration is manifested by the consistency of their sayings and the reliability of their fulfillment. It is also inspiration, a divine origin, that gives Scripture its authority.

This work of the Spirit seems to have produced two major effects in the inspired spokesperson. First, Theophilus speaks of the prophet as "instructed by God" or "taught by God." Thus, this inspiration gave them insight into divine truth by which they could speak consistently and truthfully. It is through divine inspiration that finite man is able to speak truthfully about the mysteries of the transcendent God. Second, Theophilus speaks of the prophet as "holy and righteous." Thus, this inspiration gave them a superior ethic by which they lived in the sanctification of the Spirit. In light of these two fruits of inspiration in the prophet, it makes sense why Theophilus would have seen the writings of such Spirit-inspired men as a rule of doctrine and life.

In a second passage, in his commentary on Genesis 3, Theophilus tackles a potential question from Autolycus with regards to God walking around in the garden: "You will ask me, 'You said that God must not be confined in a place; how then do you say that He walks in Paradise?'"[14] This question comes from how he had previously spoken of God as invisible and incorporeal, unlike the idols of the pagans, but now Genesis 3 says that he *walked* in the garden. This leads him to a discussion of eternal generation and the distinction between the person of the Father and of the Logos. This fascinating passage, though it does not possess the same clarity as the later fathers of the Nicene era, clearly affirms both that the Father and the Logos are eternal and that the Logos created the world, but also that they are distinct because the Logos was "generated" or "uttered" by the Father in

---

12. Grant, *Theophilus of Antioch*, II.9.
13. For his reference to the Sibyl in this category see chapter 9.
14. Grant, *Theophilus of Antioch*, II.22.

eternity.[15] This is far from the sexual reproduction of the Roman gods. The essence of his teaching is this:

> Hence the holy scriptures and all those inspired by the Spirit teach us, and one of them, John, says, "In the beginning was the Logos, and the Logos was with God." He shows that originally God was alone and the Logos was in Him. Then he says, "And the Logos was God; everything was made through Him; and apart from Him nothing was made." Since the Logos is God, and deriving his nature from God, whenever the Father of the universe wills to do so he sends him into some place where he is present and is heard and seen.[16]

In this passage, he asserts four important theological points: (1.) the Logos existed eternally with or "in" the Father; (2.) he was generated and not created; (3.) he is divine; and (4.) by him the Father created the world. He affirms this doctrine to be clearly taught in the "holy scriptures" and by "all those inspired by the Spirit (οἱ πνευματοφόροι; *hoi pneumatophoroi*[17])." In this list of "Spirit-bearing men" he includes the Apostle John, who he cites in order to prove this point. He not only here affirms the inspiration of the Scriptures, including John, he also puts the Gospel of John[18] in the same category as the Old Testament Scripture and implies that the rule for his doctrine comes from these same "holy scriptures." This passage demonstrates a summary of many of the points about Theophilus' understanding of Scripture proposed in this book.

In this passage, his argument from Scripture flows from his affirmation of the authority of Scripture, this authority flows from them all being inspired by the Spirit, and this inspiration produces a consistent testimony among all of the biblical writers. Also, this work of the Spirit in the scriptural authors allows them to speak clearly and consistently about the

15. This was a common distinction among the Greek apologists where they referred to the internal or immanent Logos, and then to the generated Logos. Origen sought to clarify the potential confusion from this distinction by teaching eternal generation (*De Principiis* 1.2.2); Letham, "Early Trinitarianism," 99. For this distinction in Theophilus and Justin Martyr see Litfin, "Tertullian on the Trinity," 86–8.

16. Grant, *Theophilus of Antioch*, II.22.

17. This is the same word used in II.9, which Grant does not translate consistently. Here in II.22 he translates as "those inspired by the Spirit;" in II.9 where the Greek is πνευματοφόροι πνεύματος ἁγίου (*pneumatophoroi pneumatos hagiou*), he translates as "possessed by a holy Spirit."

18. He only refers to the Gospel of John and there is no evidence of a clear allusion or use of the epistles of John in AA.

mysteries of the divine "triad" and the eternal generation of the Logos. According to Theophilus, these truths are beyond the grasp of man's reason, but through the Spirit's inspiration they have been made known to man. This is an example of that first effect of inspiration seen above in which the inspired men are "taught of God" and enabled to speak divine truths that are otherwise inaccessible to man.

In another passage, Theophilus recounts the history of man and his fall into sin. He says that this presentation of human history is accurate and truthful because it is an account inspired by the Holy Spirit: "All these things are taught us by the Holy Spirit which spoke through Moses and the other prophets; so that the writings which belong to us, the worshippers of God, are proved to be more ancient, but also more true, than all historians and poets."[19] Here he asserts that the Old Testament was able to get the story of creation right because it was revealed to its writers by the Holy Spirit. As Parsons points out,

> Theophilus's explicit theory of inspiration added credibility to his rhetorical moves. His judicial rhetoric so often relied on the consistent testimony of the biblical writers who functioned as friendly witnesses in the court of opinion. Lest his audience assume that his consistency claims worked merely by guile, he provided a theory of inspiration that explained how his witnesses could be so thoroughly consistent.[20]

For this reason, Theophilus says that the Bible's presentation of the nature of God, the creation of the world, and the formation of man is far superior to all attempts of Greek and Roman philosophers and poets. And this is the direct result of divine inspiration: "For this reason it is plain that all the rest were in error and that only the Christians have held the truth—we who are instructed by the Holy Spirit who spoke in the holy prophets and foretold everything."[21] The truthfulness of the Christian system and its superiority comes from divine inspiration and the continual work of the Spirit in the Christian to instruct him through those divinely-inspired writings. It is because the Old Testament prophets were inspired by the Spirit that they were able to present the truth, even a truth that they didn't witness first-hand. As he later says, "How much more, then, shall we know the truth, since we learn it from the holy prophets, who were filled with the

---

19. Grant, *Theophilus of Antioch*, II.30.
20. Parsons, "Epilogue" in *Ancient Apologetic Exegesis*.
21. Grant, *Theophilus of Antioch*, II.33.

holy Spirit of God? For this reason, all the prophets spoke harmoniously and in agreement with one another when they predicted what was going to happen to the whole world."[22]

RHETORICAL STRATEGY

The doctrine of inspiration is not only affirmed plainly various times throughout his apology, but it is also noteworthy to see the important rhetorical placement of these affirmations. The doctrine of inspiration is affirmed at two key turning points in the structure of his argument, in books 2 and 3. In book 2, the structure can be summarized in this way, (1) he gives a critique of pagan philosophers, chs. 2–8 and (2) he gives a scriptural presentation of the Christian worldview that stands in antithesis to the paganism described in 2–8, chs. 9–35. We have already seen how two Scripture-saturated arguments bracket this latter section, appearing in II.10 and II.35,[23] but another structure is used that centers the whole argument for the Christian view of God, creation, and man, in two affirmations of the divine origin of scriptural revelation.[24]

In the very center of the structure of his argument where he transitions from his treatment of pagan sources to his defense of Christian literature, he begins with an affirmation of inspiration in II.9. It is fitting to quote II.9 in its entirety:

> The men of God, who were possessed by a holy Spirit and became prophets and were inspired and instructed by God himself, were taught by God and became holy and righteous. For this reason they were judged worthy to receive the reward of becoming instruments of God and containing wisdom from him. Through Wisdom they spoke about the creation of the world and about everything else; for they prophesied about pestilences and famines and wars. There were not just one or two of them but more at various times and seasons among the Hebrews, as well as the Sibyl among the Greeks.[25] All of them were consistent with one another and with themselves, and they described events which had previously occurred, events in their own time, and events which are now being fulfilled in our times. For this reason we are persuaded that their

---

22. Grant, *Theophilus of Antioch*, III.17.
23. Grant, *Theophilus of Antioch*, II.10, 34–5.
24. Grant, *Theophilus of Antioch*, II.9, 33–4.
25. See chapter 9 for a discussion of the use of the Sibyl in Theophilus.

> predictions of coming events will prove correct, just as the former events took place correctly.[26]

These words on the nature of the divine inspiration of prophecy and Scripture begin his mini-commentary on Genesis.[27] However, he then concludes this section with a return to this theme. Because of the sinfulness of man and the vain speculations of philosophers, and the intervention of demons, men were not able to attain to the truth without God thus intervening and giving a revelation of himself and the world. As he says in II.33, "For this reason it is plain that all the rest were in error and that only the Christians have held the truth—we who are instructed by the Holy Spirit who spoke in the holy prophets and foretold everything."[28] In II.34 he makes the same point when he says, "The God and Father and Maker of the universe did not abandon mankind but gave a law and sent holy prophets to proclaim and to teach the human race so that each one of us might become sober and recognize that God is one."[29] Scripture-saturated arguments and an affirmation of divine inspiration form an *inclusio* around his positive presentation of the Christian faith. And, the affirmation of inspiration in II.9 serves as the pivot point by which he ends his critique of pagan philosophy and begins his claim for the superiority of Christianity. The Scriptures are the bookends that structure his argument and are the axle around which the whole revolves.

By noting this structure, it shows that inspiration is a foundational idea for Theophilus' worldview. It is actually the source of the Christian's understanding of God, the world, and his own place in it. Without this inspired word given by God, the Jews and Christians would have gone the way of the errors of the rest of the nations. It is due to their access to the consistent and authoritative inspiration of the Holy Spirit in the Scriptures that the Christians have such a superior worldview.

Book three also has a similar structure that places inspiration at the center. As Parsons has noted,

---

26. Grant, *Theophilus of Antioch*, II.9.

27. McVey describes the commentary in this way, which is helpful for understanding it in its apologetic context: "Theophilus's treatment of Genesis 1–3 is not a systematic, verse-by-verse commentary, but as befits its literary context, an apologetic argument, designed to address the question of its truth in the light of contemporaneous philosophical and proto-scientific thought;" McVey, "Use of Stoic Cosmogony," 58.

28. Grant, *Theophilus of Antioch*, II.33.

29. Grant, *Theophilus of Antioch*, II.34.

"Through One and the Same Spirit"

His concept of inspiration supports the unity of his third letter. For Theophilus, divine inspiration of the prophets explains both the superiority of their ethics which he argued in [AA] 3.9–15, and the superiority of their chronology which he argued in [AA] 3.16–30. His thoughts about inspiration therefore fittingly appear near the border of these two major portions of the letter, in [AA] 3.17.[30]

Book three has two main arguments: (1) the consistency of the Christian ethic (III.9–15), and (2) the antiquity of Christianity (III.16–30). He uses the doctrine of inspiration as a fulcrum that connects and balances these two arguments. Reminiscent of the same structure in book II, in III.17 he says,

> How much more, then, shall we know the truth, since we learn it from the holy prophets, who were filled with the holy Spirit of God? For this reason all the prophets spoke harmoniously and in agreement with one another when they predicted what was going to happen to the whole world. The very outcome of the previously predicted and fulfilled events can teach those who love learning—or rather, love truth—that their proclamations are really true, those which were made concerning the times and seasons before the deluge and the number of years from the creation of the world up to the present.[31]

These structures demonstrate that the idea of inspiration is not merely peripheral to Theophilus' thinking, something that he mentions in passing, but it has a foundational and central role in his thought and the structure of his apology. As has been seen, citations and allusions that span major portions of his canon are the foundation of individual arguments in II.10, II.35, and III.11–14, and his affirmations of inspiration often appear at key places in his rhetorical structure. Clearly, therefore, the inspired Scriptures are foundational to his thought and his apology. If one misses this point, he misses the very nature of Theophilus' argument and the case he is making for the Christian worldview.

---

30. Parsons, *Ancient Apologetic Exegesis*, ch. 4.
31. Grant, *Theophilus of Antioch*, III.17.

PART 2 | THEOPHILUS' DOCTRINE OF SCRIPTURE

SCRIPTURE'S INSPIRATION AND THE SECOND CENTURY

Theophilus is not alone in his affirmation of divine inspiration among the Christian writers of the second century.[32] Clement of Rome, for example, also affirmed the divine nature of Scripture and makes an important deduction from it—truthfulness or inerrancy: "You have looked into the holy scriptures, which *are* true, which *were given* by the Holy Spirit. You know that nothing unrighteous or falsified is written in them."[33] Justin Martyr likewise affirms the divine inspiration of the prophets,[34] though he does have a particular nuance in which he focuses on the activity of the Logos in this inspiration.[35]

An earlier contemporary of Theophilus, Athenagoras of Athens, also makes a clear affirmation about the necessity of revelation and the superiority of Christian revelation since it comes from the Spirit of God.

> For poets and philosophers, as to other subjects so also to this, have applied themselves in the way of conjecture, moved, by reason of their affinity with the afflatus from God, each one by his own soul, to try whether he could find out and apprehend the truth; but they have not been found competent fully to apprehend it, because they thought fit to learn, not from God concerning God, but each one from himself; hence they came each to his own conclusion respecting God, and matter, and forms, and the world. But we have for witnesses of the things we apprehend and believe, prophets, men who have pronounced concerning god and the things of God, guided by the Spirit of God. And you too will admit, excelling all others as you do in intelligence and in piety towards the true God (τὸ ὄντως θεῖον; *to ontōs theion*), that it would be irrational for us to cease to believe in the Spirit from God, who moved the mouths

---

32. In fact, his affirmations found in this section also find parallel in Josephus: "... there is no discrepancy in what is written; seeing that, on the contrary, the prophets alone had this privilege, obtaining knowledge of the most remote and ancient history through the inspiration which they owed to God, and committing to writing a clear account of the events of their own time just as they occurred . . ." Josephus, *Contra Apion* I.37–38.

33. Clement of Rome, *First Clement* 45.2–3.

34. Justin Martyr, *First Apology*, 33–4.

35. We also saw in a previous quote of Theophilus how though the Sophia of God or the Holy Spirit is more consistently connected with this work of inspiration in the prophets, he does also understand the Logos to be involved in some way (II.10).

of the prophets like musical instruments, and to give heed to mere human opinions.[36]

Like Theophilus, Athenagoras shows the necessity of revelation for true knowledge of God and affirms that revelation has come to man through the Spirit. He even uses the illustration of the Holy Spirit using men as though they were musical instruments in order to play the notes that he intended. This work of the Spirit in the prophets is what gives them their reliability in what they say about God and the world, what gives them their consistency, and also what makes the Christian system superior to that of the philosophers and poets who guided their thinking by their own reason and experience. Also, for Athenagoras, it is divine inspiration that obligates the Christians to hold firmly to the Spirit-inspired words and not to abandon them in favor of mere human opinion. Like Theophilus, Athenagoras bases his claim for the divine authority and consistency of Scripture on the Spirit's inspiration. As Bingham says, "Athenagoras's metaphor, whatever else it does, does not convey the idea of an unstructured tune and he does not entertain the possibility of contradiction between the prophets. When they compose under inspiration they do so in such a way that their own text coheres and there is harmony between them."[37]

In conclusion, though these few examples do not give a comprehensive understanding of inspiration in the second century, it does demonstrate that what Theophilus affirms about the inspiring activity of the Holy Spirit is also found in some of his predecessors and contemporaries. May these few examples motivate further research into the nature of inspiration and the doctrine of Scripture in other second-century fathers.

---

36. Athenagoras, "A Plea for the Christians," in ANF 2:132, [=ch. 7]. Cf. "A Plea for the Christians," 9. For a further analysis of the idea of inspiration in Athenagoras, see Bingham, "'We Have the Prophets," 211–42.

37. Bingham, "'We Have the Prophets,'" 231.

8

"More Ancient and More Trustworthy"

Theophilus' Doctrine of the Antiquity and Consistency of Scripture

THEOPHILUS' CONCEPT OF THE inspiration of Scripture is crucial to his whole doctrine. It is the inspiration of the Spirit that ensures that the prophetic words are divine words that require faith and obedience. In other words, inspiration is the foundation of scriptural authority. However, divine authority is not the only byproduct of the work of inspiration. Theophilus also affirms that the work of the Spirit in the writers of Scripture is what makes the Christian faith "more ancient and more trustworthy" than pagan religion or philosophy. In this chapter, we will consider Theophilus' affirmations about the antiquity and consistency of Scripture and the importance of these scriptural attributes for his apology.

ANTIQUITY OF SCRIPTURE

Another key aspect of Theophilus' doctrine of Scripture is his presentation and defense of the antiquity of Scripture. The antiquity of Scripture is a key component in the apologetic defense, not only of Theophilus, but of other apologists as well.[1] As Grant points out, "To most writers and readers of

---

1. We saw this before in the affirmation of Tatian where he saw in the Scriptures something "too old to be compared with the opinions of the Greeks." Tatian, "Address of

apologetic works antiquity was, indeed, a proof of truth." It was the supposed newness of Christianity that Diognetus used to attack Christianity earlier in the second century,[2] and this was also an important point that Minucius Felix addressed in his apology, *Octavius*, which was written a couple of decades after Theophilus. The Christians at times were attacked as destroyers of tradition or inventors of novelties, but they understood themselves as the proponents of a more ancient tradition.

For example, Celsus wrote an attack on Christianity in the mid-second century in which he makes a similar argument. Celsus even made the affirmation that Christianity simply borrowed and stole from other religions.[3] Origen was the first to directly address his accusations in the mid-third century. In fact, Jean-Marie Vermande has sought to prove how at least in book 3, Theophilus is responding to this claim made by Celsus.[4] Whether he is refuting Celsus's formulation of the argument or Autolycus's own version, Theophilus certainly places great weight on the antiquity of Christianity and the antiquity of its literature.

According to III.1, demonstrating the antiquity of Scripture is one of the main purposes behind book 3: "therefore I too will not shrink from summing up for you, with God's help, the antiquity of our writings." It is in this book that he uses a chronology of the world as a defense of the antiquity of Christianity.[5] He begins his section on the chronology[6] with these words, "Now I wish with God's help to demonstrate the chronology for you more exactly, so that you may recognize that our doctrine is neither modern nor mythical but more ancient and true than all the poets and historians who wrote on what they knew nothing about."[7] This section too starts with an antithesis between the vain opinions of

---

Tatian to the Greeks," in ANF 2:77, [=ch. 29].

2. Quasten and Plumpe, eds., *The Letter to Diognetus*, 135, [=ch. 1].

3. Grant, *Greek Apologists*, 135. Though, as Grant points out, it is unlikely that Theophilus was intentionally responding to the charges of Celsus, but the reference here to Celsus does show the importance of the argument that Theophilus makes as it was a concern for more pagans than just Autolycus.

4. Vermande, "Théophile d'Antioche contre Celse; A Autolycos III," 102–23.

5. For the sources and problems associated with the text of Theophilus' chronology, see Grant, *Greek Apologists*, 155–156; Grant, "Bible of Theophilus," 189–95.

6. Cf. Grant, *Theophilus of Antioch*, III.16–29.

7. Grant, *Theophilus of Antioch*, III.16.

philosophers and poets[8] and then an affirmation of the authority and consistency of Scripture.[9]

The Christians' books have their beginning in the time of Moses and those who came out of Egypt: "These Hebrews were our forefathers, and from them we possess the sacred books which are older than all other writers, as we have already said."[10] Moses provides the most consistent and truthful account of the chronology of the world before and after the deluge because of divine inspiration. As Theophilus affirms, "We now proceed to [provide a chronology of the world], which Moses the minister of God described through the Holy Spirit."[11] Upon the conclusion of his chronology, he says, "From the compilation of the periods of time and from all that has been said, the antiquity of the prophetic writings and the divine nature of our message are obvious. This message is not recent in origin, nor are our writings, as some suppose, mythical and false. They are actually more ancient and more trustworthy."[12]

His understanding of scriptural antiquity provides supporting evidence for Scripture's authority. According to Parsons, "Theophilus claimed that their [the Christians'] books were more ancient (and thus more trustworthy and therefore more authoritative, according to Greco-Roman literary standards) than the writings of the historians and poets."[13] It is actually the divine inspiration that produced the Scriptures which allowed for a trustworthy account of ancient history before the prophets were born. As he says in II.10,

> It was he, Spirit of God and Beginning and Sophia and Power of the Most High, who came down into the prophets and spoke through them about the creation of the world and all the rest. For the prophets did not exist when the world came into existence; there were the Sophia of God which is in him and his holy Logos who is always present with him.[14]

---

8. Grant, *Theophilus of Antioch*, III.16–21.

9. Grant, *Theophilus of Antioch*, III.17, 23–5, 29.

10. Theophilus, in contrast to many literary-critical scholars, clearly affirmed the Mosaic authorship of the Pentateuch, specifically Genesis, Exodus, and Deuteronomy all of which he cites. Cf. Grant, *Theophilus of Antioch*, III.20.

11. Grant, *Theophilus of Antioch*, III.23.

12. Grant, *Theophilus of Antioch*, III.29.

13. Parsons, *Ancient Apologetic Exegesis*, ch. 4.

14. Grant, *Theophilus of Antioch*, II.10; cf. II.31–2.

"More Ancient and More Trustworthy"

His chronology is a strategic way by which he demonstrates this point. Though he makes a few calculation mistakes, and he is wrong about Moses being 900–1000 years before the Trojan war, the point of the current book is to present his understanding not necessarily the apologetic effect. It is interesting, and not something that one would probably see in a modern-day apologetic handbook, that Theophilus uses chronology as an apologetic tool. However, understanding his rhetorical structure is key for appreciating the importance of his chronology. He spends so much time (III.16–30) on the chronology of the world in order to show that only Christian literature, inspired by God, can give an accurate account of ancient history, and it is through this that he is able to demonstrate the antiquity of the Christian religion.

Behind this affirmation is the realization that Theophilus saw Christianity, (and rightfully so), as an extension and development of Judaism.[15] Theophilus, who clearly identifies himself as a Christian, also says that the ancient children of Abraham were "our forefathers"[16] and David was "our ancestor."[17] This is in fact how the New Testament presents it as well (Gal 3:29). According to Haykin, this was "the standard answer among Christian apologists."[18] Therefore, depending on the connection between Moses and the New Testament, he shows how the Christian literature and worldview is more ancient and truer than all others. These two sets of writings, the Law and Prophets on the one hand and the Gospels and Apostles on the other, are connected both through their inspiration by the one Spirit of God and by being part of a singular story and religious tradition.

The affirmation of the antiquity of Scripture was an important aspect of Theophilus' doctrine of Scripture. It was its antiquity that supported and gave credibility to its claims to authority, and his understanding of its antiquity is connected intimately with the work of the Holy Spirit. Though the prophets were not around to witness creation and many of the pre-Flood events, they could have reliable access to them since the divine Sophia was

---

15. Bingham, "'We Have the Prophets,'" 226–7; Bingham points out this unity as an important aspect of how Athenagoras and Justin Martyr understood the prophets.

16. Grant, *Theophilus of Antioch*, III.20.

17. Grant, *Theophilus of Antioch*, III.25.

18. It is interesting to see the contrast between Theophilus' argument and that of *The Letter to Diognetus*. This anonymous letter does not defend Christianity from the charge of novelty by an appeal to its revelation in the Old Testament, rather he says that it was planned prior in the eternal counsel between the Father and his Word. Haykin, "Sharing the Faith: The Letter to Diognetus," in *Rediscovering the Church Fathers*, 49–68.

then present, and God's Sophia was the one who inspired the scriptural prophets.

CONSISTENCY OF SCRIPTURE

Theophilus of Antioch also makes the claim that the Scriptures are perfectly consistent, and it was this very fact that led to his conversion. It was this recognition that seems to have impacted him most, and therefore understandably became a central aspect of his doctrine of Scripture. When he found the Old Testament Scriptures and saw how they were being fulfilled, he believed in God and was converted. As he says,

> At that time I encountered the sacred writings of the holy prophets, who through the Spirit of God foretold past events in the way that they happened, present events in the way they are happening, and future events in the order in which they will be accomplished. Because I obtained proof from the events which took place after being predicted, I do not disbelieve but believe, in obedience to God.[19]

As seen here and elsewhere, Theophilus presents two types of scriptural consistency— (1) internal consistency (consistency proper), the consistency of one passage of Scripture with another, (2) and also external (coherence), the consistency of Scripture with the facts of history that it claims to record or foretell. He affirms both of these in II.9:

> All of them [the inspired prophets] [1] were consistent with one another and with themselves, and [2] they described events which had previously occurred, events in their own time, and events which are now being fulfilled in our times. For this reason we are persuaded that their predictions of coming events will prove correct, just as the former events took place correctly.[20]

---

19. Grant, *Theophilus of Antioch*, I.14. Ferguson has proposed that this is a parallel to *Epistle of Barnabas* 1.7, "For the Master has made known to us through the Prophets the things past and the things present and has given a foretaste to us of the things about to be; which, seeing *them* come to pass one after another, just as he said, we ought to make a richer and more sublime sacrifice in fear of him." "Parallel" is an appropriate word, since it appears unlikely to be an allusion, due to a lack of consistent verbal parallels. However, the conceptual parallel is striking and serves to show the importance of this thought for the second-century Christians. It will later be seen in Justin Martyr as well. Ferguson, "*Theophilus of Antioch*," 112.

20. Grant, *Theophilus of Antioch*, II.9.

This is in the context of Theophilus speaking of the inspired Old Testament prophets. Their inspiration is manifested in their consistency and harmony. He lists two requirements for this consistency: in reporting historical details of the past and in predicting the future. They were consistent with what they reported as history or as current events, and what they had predicted was consistent with what happened after them. Therefore, due to his confidence in their inspiration, he not only trusts their report of things past, sees the fulfillment of their words in things happening in his own day, but he also rests in them concerning what they say about the future.

As is later seen in Theophilus, he also sees this same authority in the accounts of creation and the Fall. Theophilus claims that the book of Genesis meets these standards of historical consistency. He clearly believed that Genesis 1–3 represented historical fact and not myth. As McVey has pointed out, "Although he is clearly aware of the disjunction and repetition in the two creation stories (Gen 1:1–2:4a and 2:4b–3:24), he addresses the difficulties by harmonizing the divergences to produce a single narrative. Furthermore that narrative is history, not myth."[21]

He claims that this account of creation in six days is far superior to all the attempts of philosophers to describe the creation of the world. In II.11, he cites Genesis 1:3–2:3, and then says these words in the following chapter:

> No man can adequately set forth the whole exegesis and plan of the Hexaëmeros (six day's work), even if he were to have ten thousand mouths and ten thousand tongues. Not even if he were to live ten thousand years, continuing in this life, would he be competent to say anything adequately in regard to these matters, because of the surpassing greatness and riches of the Wisdom of God to be found in this Hexaëmeros quoted above.[22]

In book II, chapters 20 and 21, he quotes all of Genesis 2 and 3. In this way he makes an application of this principle and his confidence in the inspiration of Scripture to the book of Genesis. He says that this section of Scripture "contains the words of the sacred history."[23] He clearly affirms the inspiration of this portion of Scripture and its consistency with the actual facts of what happened. He determines this faithfulness by seeing how the results of what happened in Genesis still are seen clearly in the world

---

21. McVey, "Use of Stoic Cosmogony in Theophilus," 54–5.
22. Grant, *Theophilus of Antioch*, II.12.
23. Grant, *Theophilus of Antioch*, II.20.

Part 2 | Theophilus' Doctrine of Scripture

around him: such as the effects of the Fall on serpents and childbirth.[24] For Theophilus, the Genesis account is the only one that actually answers the questions that face every generation. It is the only one that explains the world and the state in which men and women find themselves. The affirmation of Jeffrey Johnson also aptly summarizes Theophilus' own conviction presented in these chapters of his apology: "A personal God creating everything out of nothing is the *only* logical and self-consistent explanation of the origins of the universe. . . . The various explanations that man has sought to give for the origin, nature, and purpose of the universe do not hold up under their own weight. Only God's Word does not contradict itself."[25]

It is interesting, especially in light of modern historical-criticism, that Theophilus uses the first 11 chapters of Genesis as the basis for his teaching on the inspiration and superiority of Scripture. He says clearly that "Moses the minister of God described [the creation event] through the Holy Spirit."[26] For Theophilus, the facts and principles contained in Genesis regarding God, creation, man, and sin are true to history, consistent with the rest of Scriptures, and far superior to any of the inventions of the pagans.

In II.35, Theophilus looks at how Scripture is perfectly consistent on the nature of God, creation of the world, and the formation of man. He cites several passages of the Prophets and shows how they are in perfect accord with the passages of Genesis cited earlier. He says,

> It is obvious how agreeably and harmoniously all the prophets spoke, making their proclamation by one and the same spirit concerning the sole rule of God, and the origin of the world, and the making of man. . . . And why should I recount the multitude of the prophets, since they are many and made countless statements in agreement and harmony?[27]

---

24. "God made man on the sixth day but revealed his formation after the seventh day, when he also made paradise so that man might be in a better place and a finer location. Facts prove the truth of these statements. How can one fail to be aware of the pangs which women suffer in childbirth? Afterwards they forget the pain so that God's word may be fulfilled, prescribing the increase and multiplication of the human race. Or the condemnation of the serpent, which is hateful, creeping on its belly and eating dirt, so that this too may demonstrate to us the truth of what has been said?" Grant, *Theophilus of Antioch*, II.23.

25. Johnson, *Absurdity of Unbelief*, 38–9.

26. Grant, *Theophilus of Antioch*, III.23.

27. Grant, *Theophilus of Antioch*, II.35.

Due to his understanding of the inspiration of Scripture, Theophilus also sees the Scriptures as perfectly consistent and harmonious. The Scriptures are perfectly consistent with each other (internally) because they are inspired by "one and the same Spirit." They cannot contradict each other because behind the human authors there is a single divine Spirit that is speaking through each of them.[28]

These passages speak of the consistency found within the Old Testament, however Theophilus also says that this consistency and harmony extends to the Gospels. Speaking specifically of the ethical principles found in the Bible, he says, "Furthermore, concerning the justice of which the law spoke, the teaching of the prophets and the gospels is consistent with it because all the inspired men made utterances by means of the one Spirit of God."[29] This passage not only affirms the consistency between the Old Testament and the Gospels, but it also says that the same Spirit that inspired the Old Testament inspired the Gospels, and, therefore, he puts the Gospels on the same level as the Old Testament, at least with respect to inspiration. It is divine inspiration that makes the Scriptures consistent. Though it is not clear which Gospels he has in mind in this place, he does cite John 1 as explicitly from the Spirit, in III.13–14 he cites various passages from Matthew, and he also uses Luke 18:27 in his discussion of the Logos.[30]

Also, though he does not here include the Epistles, in III.14 he cites a passage from Rom 13 and from First Timothy 2 and refers to them as "the divine word" (ὁ θεῖος λόγος; *ho theios logos*). He presents the teaching of these letters, being the divine word, as presenting a consistent ethical system to that found in the Law, prophets, and Gospels. In this way it is plain that Theophilus understood that the Scriptures were consistent—Law,

---

28. Though the poets and philosophers sometimes spoke certain truths, they are borrowing from the law and prophets. "And willing or unwilling they made declarations about the conflagration of the world in harmony with the prophets, though they were much more recent and stole these things from the Law and prophets;" Grant, *Theophilus of Antioch*, II.37. Also, Haykin, in his affirmation about the role of Scripture in Irenaeus's critique of Gnosticism, said that Irenaeus had a similar understanding of inspiration and inerrancy: "Just as it is impossible to conceive of Christ ever uttering falsehood, so the writings of his authorized representatives are incapable of error. This quality of absolute truthfulness can also be predicated of the authors of the books of the Old Testament, since the Spirit who spoke through the apostles also spoke through the Old Testament authors;" Haykin, *Giving Glory to the Consubstantial Trinity*, 51.

29. Grant, *Theophilus of Antioch*, III.12.

30. Grant, *Theophilus of Antioch*, II.10.

Part 2 | Theophilus' Doctrine of Scripture

Prophets, Gospels, and Epistles—because they were all inspired by "one and the same Spirit."

Consistency not only means that the Scriptures are consistent among all of their parts, but it also means that the Scriptures are accurate and truthful with their presentation of facts and events. Up to this point, I have called this type of consistency, external consistency or coherence. However, this aspect could be better defined as a form of inerrancy.[31]

Theophilus argues in this way: (1.) The Christian Scriptures are inspired by the Holy Spirit, (2a.) therefore Scriptures are superior to the prophets and poets of the pagans,[32] (2b.) they are consistent with themselves among all their parts, (2c.) and they are truthful and without error regarding their propositions about the past, present, or the future. He makes this very argument in III.17:

> Furthermore, it is said that there were diviners and seers at the time of the historians, and that people who learned from them wrote accurate histories. [2a] How much more, then, shall we know the truth, since we learn it from the holy prophets, [1] who were filled with the holy Spirit of God? [2b] For this reason all the prophets spoke harmoniously and in agreement with one another when they predicted what was going to happen to the whole world. [2c] The very outcome of the previously predicted and fulfilled events can teach those who love learning—or rather, love truth—that their proclamations are really true, those which were made concerning the times and seasons before the deluge and the number of years from the creation of the world up to the present. [2a] This will demonstrate the nonsensical falsehood of the historians and show that their statements are not true.[33]

The Scriptures are superior to the pagan prophets, perfectly consistent with themselves, and they are "really true." If the blind pagan prophets were able to stumble upon the truth every once in a while, how much more would the prophets inspired by the Spirit of God be thoroughly true and inerrant.

---

31. Paul D. Feinberg in his article, "The Meaning of Inerrancy," says, "Inerrancy means that when all facts are known, the Scriptures in their original autographs and properly interpreted will be shown to be wholly true in everything that they affirm, whether that has to do with doctrine or morality or with the social, physical, or life science." Cf. Feinberg, "The Meaning of Inerrancy," in *Inerrancy*, ed. Norman Geisler, 294.

32. Note the *inclusio* with 2a that he uses to emphasize what it is that makes the Christian's system so distinct from and superior to the Greek poets, philosophers, and historians.

33. Grant, *Theophilus of Antioch*, III.17.

This is a conclusion that he derives from his understanding of the nature of Scripture: since the Scriptures are inspired by the Spirit, and since the Spirit cannot be wrong because he is one with God, then the Scriptures also must be consistent and inerrant, or in his own words, "really true." Though he does not use the modern term of inerrancy and we must be careful of reading our own theological convictions into the language of the ancient writer, Theophilus is affirming in this passage that all that the Scriptures said by the singular Spirit of God is "really true" and perfectly consistent.

At the end of Book II, he includes some quotations from Greek philosophers that serve to confirm the truth that is taught in Scripture. However, his understanding of their access to this truth is either by the over-powering nature of truth or an active borrowing from Scripture. In II.37 he affirms, "willing or unwillingly they [the poets and philosophers] made declarations . . . in harmony with the prophets, though they were much more recent and stole these things from the law and the prophets." In II.38 he says, "All of them said these things [about providence and judgement in harmony with Scripture], for they were convinced by the truth." However, it is only the Scriptures that provide a consistent source for these truths—"a pledge of the truth." The philosophers and poets at times recognize them, but at other points they deny the same truths; however, Scripture is perfectly consistent. As he says, "So even though the [Greek and Roman] writers spoke of gods, they ended with monotheism; though they denied providence they also spoke of providence; though they said there was no judgement they admitted that there will be a judgement; those who denied the existence of sensation after death [i.e., resurrection] also admitted it."[34]

Though the philosophers occasionally affirmed certain truths also taught in Scripture, like Plato's affirmation of the oneness of God,[35] they are drops of honey mixed with poison. The consistency of Scripture is a key argument in Theophilus' rhetoric. This conviction reflects the third important positive argument in ancient rhetoric ('consistency of testimony'), and his critique of the consistency of the poets and philosophers is an example of the negative arguments recommended by Cicero.[36] The consistency of Scripture among all the prophets is the basis for his Scripture-saturated

---

34. Grant, *Theophilus of Antioch*, II.38.
35. Grant, *Theophilus of Antioch*, III.7.
36. Parsons, "By One and the Same Spirit," 40–41. Cf. chapter 1 of this book.

Part 2 | Theophilus' Doctrine of Scripture

arguments on creation,[37] the oneness of God,[38] and ethics.[39] However, he also turns the tables on his opponent by pointing out the great inconsistency of the philosophers and poets.[40] He says,

> All these, as lovers of empty and useless fame, neither knew the truth themselves nor impelled others toward the truth. The very things they said convict them: their statements are inconsistent and most of them demolished their own doctrines. They not only refuted one another but in some instances even nullified their own doctrines so that their fame ended in dishonor and foolishness; for they are condemned by intelligent persons.[41]

Even the best philosophers among the Greeks, such as Plato, were guilty of great inconsistencies with respect to ethical principles[42] and the immortality of the human soul.[43] Only Scripture, due to its divine source, provides a coherent and consistent understanding of the world, including the nature of being (ontology), truth (epistemology), and ethics.

However, though he sees the Scriptures as true and infallible, he does not see his own writings as such. After giving a very interesting chronology of the world, he recognizes that he is probably close, but he may have erred in some place.[44] However, he does not ever blame the Scriptures for these errors.[45] The potential errors in his chronology come from his own calculations and not the Scriptures. This fact can be seen elsewhere as he never attributes error to the Scripture, nor does he ever set himself or another source as a corrector or judge of Scripture. The authority, inspiration, and consistency of Scripture are foundational for his arguments and his apologetic.

---

37. Grant, *Theophilus of Antioch*, II.10.
38. Grant, *Theophilus of Antioch*, II.35.
39. Grant, *Theophilus of Antioch*, III.11–5.
40. Grant, *Theophilus of Antioch*, II.3–8.
41. Grant, *Theophilus of Antioch*, III.3.
42. Grant, *Theophilus of Antioch*, III.6.
43. Grant, *Theophilus of Antioch*, III.7.
44. Though he certainly saw himself as a speaker of truth in accordance with Scripture and with the aid and influence of the Holy Spirit, he does not place himself in the same category as Scripture, Old or New Testaments. Thus, Rogers seems to overstate the case when he says, "Apparently, when it comes to nomos there is a chain of prophet-like teachers who are all informed by the Logos of God, perhaps even Theophilus himself as he formulates an appropriate invitation to Autolycus;" Rogers, "Theophilus of Antioch," 222.
45. Grant, *Theophilus of Antioch*, III.29.

Scripture's Consistency and the Second Century

Theophilus was not alone in his affirmations of the consistency and harmony of Scripture. *The Epistle of Barnabas*, towards the beginning of the second century, made a similar affirmation concerning the external consistency or coherence of scriptural prophecy: "For the Master has made known to us through the Prophets the things past and the things present and has given a foretaste to us of the things about to be; which, seeing *them* come to pass one after another, just as he said, we ought to make a richer and more sublime sacrifice in fear of him."[46] According to Barnabas, this consistency of the prophetic witness should lead us to a more profound trust and a greater fear of God.

Justin Martyr also made a similar argument by an appeal to the coherence of scriptural declarations with their fulfillment:

> But lest anyone should argue against us, what excludes [the reasoning] that He who is called by us Christ, a man born of men, performed what we call His mighty works by magical art, and by this appeared to be Son of God?—we will now offer proof, not trusting in mere assertions, but being of necessity persuaded by those who prophesied [these things] before they happened, for with our own eyes we see things that have happened and are happening just as they were predicted; and this will, we think, appear to you the strongest and surest evidence.[47]

Likewise, Irenaeus, who wrote shortly after and even used Theophilus, also affirms the harmony of all of Scripture together (internal consistency), as does Theophilus. This understanding of Scripture is key in his refutation of Gnosticism. He says, "[W]e will find that all the Scripture given us by God harmonizes, and the parables harmonize with the things that are expressly stated, and the plain statements explain the parables. Thus, through the many voices of the passages there will be heard among us one harmonious melody that hymns praises to God who made all things."[48] The Gnostics tended to use obscurer passages such as the parables to defend

---

46. *Epistle of Barnabas*, 1.7. Ferguson has pointed out the parallel between this passage and what Theophilus says in I.14; Ferguson, "*Theophilus of Antioch*," 112. Whether he is alluding to Barnabas or not, this affirmation still shows how this was a common belief among the second-century fathers.

47. St. Justin Martyr, *St. Justin Martyr: The First and Second Apologies*, 43: [=*First Apology* ch. 30]. Cf. Melito of Sardis, *On Faith*, ANF 8:756–7.

48. Irenaeus, *Against Heresies*, ed. Dillon, 88–9, [=II.28.3].

Part 2 | Theophilus' Doctrine of Scripture

their false teachings. However, for Irenaeus, no biblical text could rightly be used to contradict another for they all harmonize together as a glorious chorus that sings the praises of God.

Like Theophilus, Scripture in Irenaeus has a key rhetorical role that establishes and undergirds his whole argument, as Haykin has pointed out,

> Foundational to Irenaeus' refutation of Gnosticism are the Scriptures, the Old and the New Testaments, which, in the view of the pastor of Lyons, are both the work of the one true God. For Irenaeus, these Scriptures are perfect texts because they had been spoken by the Word of God and his Spirit (*Against Heresies* 2.28.2). The human authors of the various books of Scripture had been given perfect knowledge by the Holy Spirit and thus were incapable of proclaiming error (*Against Heresies* 3.1.1).[49]

Likewise, Parsons makes this connection between Theophilus' understanding of the consistency of Scripture in connection with inspiration and the same connection also found in Irenaeus and other writers:

> Irenaeus of Lyons was another early Christian writer who believed that there is a conceptual unity binding all of the inspired texts. This stated theology of inspiration of his, that one Spirit of God inspired both prophets and inspired Christian writers, with the result that all of the inspired texts are consistent with one another, was a traditional early Christian theology of inspiration.[50]

In conclusion, it has been demonstrated that Scripture has a key role in the thought and apologetic of Theophilus. In fact, he has a high view of Scripture that places it as the very basis and unifying principle of his whole worldview and apologetic argument. In this way and with many of his particular affirmations, he is in line with other second-century church fathers. However, there is one further aspect of his doctrine of Scripture that needs to be addressed—his use of non-canonical works. It is this point that the next chapter will address.

---

49. Haykin, *Giving Glory to the Consubstantial Trinity*, 50. cf. Irenaeus, *Against Heresies*, 3.5.1.

50. Parsons, "By One and the Same Spirit," 250–1.

9

Theophilus' Use of Non-Canonical Writings

As has been demonstrated, not only did Theophilus have a high view of Scripture, seeing it as authoritative, inspired, consistent, and the most ancient source of truth, but his affirmations find parallels in other church fathers from the second century. To fully understand Theophilus' doctrine of Scripture in his own terms one must examine the few but significant allusions and citations that are made to books that are not traditionally considered to be part of the biblical canon, especially from a Protestant perspective. This reality poses some difficulty. Though he is similar to his contemporaries in having a high view of Scripture, he is also characteristic of that period in his use of non-canonical Christian and Jewish sources.

Many modern scholars have wrestled with the problem of the use of works that came to be recognized as non-canonical and its implications for an understanding of the canon in the second century. Some church fathers of the second and third century also revered the writings of Clement, the *Shepherd of Hermas,* the *Epistle of Barnabas* and other writings as important for Christians and sometimes as part of Scripture. There have been many proposals for how this could have happened when these books were not later recognized in the more formal canon lists of the fourth century. Were these non-canonical works like the *Shepherd of Hermas*, the *Epistle of*

Part 2 | Theophilus' Doctrine of Scripture

Barnabas, and others from the Old Testament Apocrypha and pseudepigrapha given "temporary canonicity"?[1] Or, did they have a "transient authority"? Some scholars have proposed that the earliest generations had a much broader understanding of inspiration and Scripture, which then began to decline in the fourth century when the canon was finally limited to certain books.[2]

Lee McDonald's argument is characteristic of these scholars when he says, "The Christian community believed that God continued to inspire individuals in their proclamation, *just as* God inspired the writers of the New Testament literature. They believed the Spirit was the gift of God to the whole church, not just its writers of sacred literature."[3] Due to this ongoing character of the Spirit's activity, some writers may have also seen post-apostolic works as scriptural or may have even considered their own works in this way. Likewise, Allert, after pointing out one way in which inspiration is a criterion for canonicity (i.e., since all orthodox works are considered inspired), he says, "Thus, from another perspective it is incorrect to say that inspiration functioned as a criterion of canonicity if we mean by that that inspiration was believed to have been the possession of *only* the documents that later became part of the New Testament canon."[4]

Theophilus' work provides a helpful case study of this reality. One of the critiques that a reviewer has made of Parsons' important work on the rhetorical use of Scripture in Theophilus is that he fails fully to take into account his use of non-canonical Scripture.[5] Grant also says, "In his

---

1. Metzger, *Canon of the New Testament*, 165–89.

2. For approaches to the use of non-canonical Scripture in other second-century fathers, see Bingham, "Senses of Scripture in the Second Century," 26–55; Charlesworth, McDonald, and Jurgens, eds. *Sacra Scriptura: How "Non-Canonical" Texts Functioned in Early Judaism and Early Christianity*, 20–2; Beatrice, "The 'Gospel According to the Hebrews' in the Apostolic Fathers," 147–95.

3. McDonald and Sanders, eds. *The Canon Debate*, 438. Cf. Bruce, *The Canon of Scripture*, 280–3. Emphasis added.

4. Allert, *High View of Scripture?*, 59. Emphasis original.

5. Poirier, "Stuart Parsons: *Ancient Apologetic Exegesis*": "A second problem is that Parsons repeatedly uses the term 'inspired words' as a category of Theophilus' understanding of Scripture, but there is room to argue (and others *have* argued it) that Theophilus held *all* (or at least most) writings to have been inspired by *some* higher power, with Christian writings (both scriptural and non-scriptural) being those that were inspired by the Christian God. (Theophilus wrote in a day when all poetry was presumed to have been inspired. He simply extended this premise to more writings.) To refer to the words of Scripture as 'inspired' as though that marked them in some *categorical* way as Scripture is therefore misleading. Of course, it might be possible to argue against the 'all

Theophilus' Use of Non-Canonical Writings

theological system Theophilus depends *almost* entirely on the Greek Old Testament and on the books which were coming to be regarded as the New Testament."[6] This statement is in line with the thesis of this book, but the word "almost" is what now requires further attention.

First of all, the conclusion about the doctrine of Scripture in Theophilus that we have developed so far is not affected by the use of non-canonical[7] writings, since his understanding of the nature of these books would be the same if he saw them as canonical Scripture. That is to say, his understanding of the nature of his canon remains as established even though the boundary lines might be blurry, and it remains even if it excluded books held as canonical today or included books that are rejected today. Understanding his view of the nature of the canon does not totally depend upon him having the exact same canon as the modern Protestant Christian. Thus, the main purpose of this book (determine the doctrine of Scripture according to Theophilus) is not thwarted by the presence of non-canonical works in his writings. This chapter seeks to look at the extent to which Theophilus would apply this doctrine to other books outside of the known canon. Which non-canonical works did Theophilus use? Did he see them as of equal authority as the other Scriptures? How broad is his understanding of inspiration?

In this chapter, we analyze the presence of citations or allusions to extra-canonical works in Theophilus. A *citation* refers to a passage that is explicitly quoted and attributed to a particular source. With this definition, the only Christian or Jewish source outside the Old and New Testaments that is cited is the Sibyl, who is viewed by Theophilus as neither Jewish nor Christian but a singular case of God's prophetic activity among the Greeks.

On the other hand, an *allusion* is a little harder to nail down.[8] G. K Beale has provided this basic definition of an allusion: "The telltale key

---

writings are inspired' thesis—my point is that Parsons first must do this if he wants to use 'inspired words' in a way that approximates modern sensibilities to that term."

6. Grant, "Theophilus of Antioch to Autolycus," 254. Emphasis added.

7. The use of the term non-canonical, from a definitive and exclusive perspective of the canon, is anachronistic. However, the present author is using the term to refer to those books which became known as the canon of the Old Testament and New Testament, and also which at that time, from an ontological perspective, were already canonical, and thus its use is not completely anachronistic. Cf. Kruger, "The Definition of the Term 'Canon': Exclusive or Multi-Dimensional?," 1–20.

8. As Beale says, "Recognizing allusions is like interpretation: there are degrees of probability and possibility in any attempt to identify an allusion." Beale, *Handbook on the New Testament Use of the Old Testament*, 32.

to discerning an allusion is that of recognizing an *incomparable or unique parallel in wording, syntax, concept, or cluster of motifs in the same order or structure*."[9] Richard Hays and others have proposed seven criteria for the identification of allusions, specifically in the context of the New Testament's use of the Old Testament.[10] There are five of these criteria that are useful for the study of Theophilus. First, *availability*: the possible source must have been available to Theophilus. Second, *volume*: there must be significant verbal or syntactical parallels. Third, *thematic coherence*: there must be a thematic coherence and contextual appropriateness for the possible allusion. Fourth, *historical plausibility*: it must be appropriate for the historical context of Theophilus. Fifth, *satisfaction*: it must satisfy any attempt to arrive at the original meaning of Theophilus. Hays' criterion of the history of interpretation does not apply as well to Theophilus as it does the New Testament since there is not as long of a history of interpretation of Theophilus. Also, his criterion of recurrence is difficult to apply to Theophilus given our limited access to his writings, thus making it impossible to analyze other ways he might have alluded to a source since the given passage may likely be the only extant example.

CHRISTIAN AND APOCRYPHAL WORKS

Theophilus seems to be familiar with some Old Testament and New Testament Apocryphal literature and other sources as well.[11] In recent academic literature, there have been various proposals for allusions to various Christian works of the second century. Some of these proposals have more weight than others, and some may represent a common apologetic context and not literary dependence. For example, Everett Ferguson has proposed three parallels to the *Epistle of Barnabas* and one to the *Letter to Diognetus*. These appear to be conceptual parallels due to common themes in

---

9. Beale, *Handbook on the New Testament Use of the Old Testament*, 31. Emphasis original.

10. Hays, *Echoes of Scripture in the Letters of Paul*, 29–32. The full seven are: (1) availability, (2) volume, (3) recurrence, (4) thematic Coherence, (5) historical Plausibility, (6) history of Interpretation, and (7) satisfaction. Cf. Beale, *Handbook on the New Testament Use of the Old Testament*, 32–3.

11. See Appendix 1 for a list of such allusions and citations.

Theophilus' Use of Non-Canonical Writings

second-century literature and apology and lack the necessary verbal parallels that would make them allusions.[12]

The *Kerygma Petri* fr. 3 appears in an allusion in I.14, "In any case, however, they too foretold the punishments to come upon the ungodly and the incredulous, so that these punishments might be attested to all and no one might say, '*We did not hear nor did we know*'" (italics added to mark the allusion). However, he does not appear to use this work for an authoritative purpose, but rather due to its common intention of showing how God has left all men without excuse by making them aware of the coming judgment. In the context, Theophilus is making the point that though Scripture speaks consistently on the nature of judgement, there have been glimpses of this truth in other writings as well, even Greek philosophers. Though the judgement announced in Scripture also appears in some of the writings of the philosophers, Theophilus believes it is because they "stole them from the holy scriptures in order to make their own teaching seem trustworthy."[13] For this reason, both Greeks and those who have the holy scriptures have heard the announcement of a future judgement and are therefore without excuse. For this reason, his use of *Kerygma Petri* may be yet another external testimony that confirms the consistent witness of Scripture. This text is also cited by Clement of Alexandria a few decades after Theophilus:

> In the Preaching of Peter the Lord says: I chose out you twelve, judging you to be disciples worthy of me, whom the Lord willed, and thinking you faithful apostles; sending you unto the world to preach the Gospel to men throughout the world, that they should know that there is one God; to declare by faith in me [the Christ] what shall be, that they that have heard and believed may be saved, and *that they which have not believed* may hear and bear witness, *not having any defence* so as to say '*We did not hear*'.[14]

Just like Theophilus, Clement uses this passage because of its affirmation of how the clarity of the biblical message leaves its recipients without an excuse. The citation in Clement appears to connect this ministry of removing all excuses to the apostles. It is possible that Theophilus' allusion to this text may show how he viewed himself in continuity with this apostolic ministry. For this reason, he sought to present the truth of his faith and the

---

12. Ferguson, "*Theophilus of Antioch: Ad Autolycum*," 112.

13. Grant, *Theophilus of Antioch*, I.14.

14. Clement of Alexandria, *Stromata* 6.6; James, *The Apocryphal New Testament*, 17. Italics are used to mark what is shared with Theophilus.

coming judgement with abundant evidence so that Autolycus might also be left without excuse and be drawn to believe God before that dreadful day.

Theophilus also potentially uses First and Second Esdras for some historical facts about the Persian period in III.25 and 29. However, this does not give them any more authority than the other histories he cites, like Josephus or other Greek and Roman sources. In fact, it is noteworthy that Theophilus' chronology of the ancient world derived from his sacred books ends with Cyrus and the return from Babylon. In III.26 he concludes saying "It is obvious how our sacred writings are proved to be more ancient and more true than the writings of Greeks and Egyptians or any other historiographers."[15] Rhetorically, Theophilus' "sacred writings" provide him a faithful chronology of the world from creation to the time of Cyrus. Evidence of the Hebrew canon in the time of the early church suggests that Chronicles, which ends with this decree of Cyrus as the fulfillment of Jeremiah's prophecy (2 Chron 36:22–23), was the final book.[16] This would explain why Theophilus ends his sacred history with Cyrus. In this way, Theophilus' historical account of the times of the world is a canonical chronology.

Cyrus concludes the central part of his chronology, but in order to avoid accusations of partiality or neglect he continues with a brief narrative of the times from Cyrus to his own days. He says, "So that it may not be thought that I have presented matters down to Cyrus but am neglecting the subsequent periods as being unable to provide evidence, by God's help I shall try to set forth as well as possible an orderly account of the rest of the times."[17] However, this latter history is not central to his argument and appears mainly to avoid potential counterarguments. It focuses on Roman history, and he identifies his source as a scribe of Marcus Aurelius named Chryseros the Nomenclator (III.27). In light of this, it is noteworthy that he does not mention the history included in Second-Temple literature, especially historical books like First and Second Maccabees. His sacred history seems limited to the canonical story of Genesis to Chronicles. It is also important to recognize that the New Testament history does not appear in his chronology of the world. However, this is probably due to the

---

15. Grant, *Theophilus of Antioch*, III.26.

16. Beckwith, *Old Testament Canon of the New Testament Church*, 115, 123; Dempster, "'An Extraordinary Fact:' Part 2," 210–4.

17. Grant, *Theophilus of Antioch*, III.26.

Theophilus' Use of Non-Canonical Writings

lack of significant chronological information found in the New Testament writings.

In I.4 there appears to be an allusion to Second Maccabees 7:28 where he says, "God made everything out of what did not exist." If we consider the criteria for an allusion, it is possible that Theophilus would have had access to Second Maccabees (*availability*). He shows familiarity with Jewish literature in general, and also frequently reflects the Septuagint tradition that may have included this book (*historical plausibility*). However, the point made in the previous paragraph may serve as evidence against this. This passage has stronger verbal parallels than other proposals (*volume*), though an inverted order:

ὅτι οὐκ ἐξ ὄντων ἐποίησεν αὐτὰ ὁ θεὸς (2 Macc 7:28)[18]	τὰ πάντα ὁ Θεὸς ἐποίησεν ἐξ οὐκ ὄντων εἰς τὸ εἶναι. (I.4)
hoti ouk ex ontōn epoiēsen auta ho theos	*ta panta ho theos epoiēsen ex ouk ontōn eis to einai.*
Because, not of things existing did God make them.[19]	God made everything out of what did not exist.[20]

Theophilus puts "God" first in the clause while Maccabees has it at the end. They both use the same verbal form and the same basic prepositional phrase. However, the language is slightly different. Theophilus says "out of what did not exist" while Maccabees says, "not of things existing." It is not a citation, but it is possible that the combination of verbal parallels may indicate an allusion. Third, these two passages also share a similar context where creation itself is declaring how God is the creator of all things out of nothing (*coherence*). It appears to meet the five criteria for an allusion that were established above.

Another even clearer extra-biblical allusion is found in III.30 in reference to persecution: "they have appointed *prizes and honours for those who euphoniously insult God.*" The words in italics are also found in Justin's *First Apology*, 4.9. This seems to reflect a shared apologetic context, and may also indicate that Theophilus developed his arguments following the example of other apologists of his day.

---

18. Citation from Kappler, *Maccabaeorum Liber* II, 2 Mac 7:28.
19. Author's translation.
20. Grant, *Theophilus of Antioch*, I.4.

Part 2 | Theophilus' Doctrine of Scripture

The references in the table of Appendix 1 to Baruch (III.11) and First Clement (II.14) are too weak to warrant much consideration. They do not seem to meet the criteria for *volume* (2) or *satisfaction* (5).

It is very likely that Theophilus was aware of some of the Apocryphal books, and that he had a regard for the writings of his Christian contemporaries and predecessors. It is likewise possible that Theophilus' book of Jeremiah may have included Baruch, or that other Apocryphal works were included as well, such as Second Maccabees. However, there is no definitive statement about the authority of these books. The only argument for their authority in his theology is the fact that they are used at all. This is definitely something to be considered, especially in light of the rhetorical significance of allusions in other parts of Theophilus. However, the infrequency and the places in which they appear, do not require the conclusion that Theophilus saw these books as of the same divine inspiration and authority as the rest of the "divine Scriptures." In fact, they do not appear in his Scripture-saturated arguments nor in the important turning points of his rhetorical structure as the canonical Scriptures do. These allusions to these works, in conjunction with his overwhelming dependence on the Scriptures, does serve to bolster the argument made by Parsons:

> More specifically, in this study I will argue that Theophilus was able to combine his vast knowledge of the Jewish and Christian inspired texts *with his deep awareness of exegetical and early Christian apologetic traditions* in order to produce an organized, coherent, faithful, and as measured by the rhetorical standards of his own day, formidable defense of Christianity.[21]

In conclusion, Hill's affirmation concerning the second century in general is fitting for Theophilus:

> That there was variation, beyond the "core" books, and at least no successful, far-reaching attempt to impose any strict limitation, accompanied by the promulgation of authoritative lists, has been widely interpreted to mean that there was no conception at all of Scripture as a definite or closed set of books. The evidence shows, however, not the absence of a notion of delimitation but rather a level of disagreement or simply uncertainty about what belonged in that delimited body of writings.[22]

---

21. Parsons, "By One and the Same Spirit," 3. Emphasis added.
22. Hill, "'The Truth above All Demonstration,'" 67.

Theophilus' Use of Non-Canonical Writings

The church was still on its way to clarity and greater consensus on the limits of the biblical canon in the second century.[23] To a certain degree this phenomenon can be seen in Theophilus, with some books not being used (e.g., First John, Second John, Third John, Jude) and some non-canonical books being included by way of allusion. However, many of the allusions that can be mentioned are too weak to have full certainty of direct literary dependence, and they are never given *explicit* divine authority. Even if he did affirm these books to be divine in other writings or teachings, this would only serve to demonstrate the blurry lines of the formal canon that existed in the second century; but his understanding of the doctrine of Scripture as established in this book would still remain.

"THE SIBYL AMONG THE GREEKS"

Another problem that is not unique to Theophilus is his use of the Sibyl.[24] In Greek and Roman culture, the Sibyl was a female oracle who received ecstatic revelations from the gods that were used to interpret prodigies or predict the outcome of wars. Some of these oracles have become famous and there were even books of Roman oracles held at Rome and used periodically in the final centuries of the Roman Republic. Between 200 BC and 150 AD, Jews and Christians adapted this style of literature and the importance that it had in pagan culture to create their own oracular literature under the name of the Greek sibyls. This literature, particularly book 3,[25] seeks to rebuke pagan culture for its immorality, speak to them about the true God, call them to repentance, and warn them of judgement. Some of the oracles also were presented as prophecies of Christ.[26] Upon comparing their use by Jews and Christians, John Collins has affirmed that "They had

---

23. The use of these sources in Theophilus can be easily explained, as briefly done here, but this is not to be expected in every early church father. Though Theophilus is representative in many ways, there are other fathers that make much more extensive use of non-canonical works. For example, Clement of Alexandria provides a much stronger case for those who want to argue that these books were considered as canonical and equal to Scripture in the second century.

24. One of the standard works on the Sibyl is that by Jane Lightfoot; Lightfoot, *The Sibylline Oracles*.

25. Gruen, "Jews, Greeks, and Romans in the Third Sibylline Oracle," 451–72.

26. Cf. *Sybilline Oracles*, books 6–8.

Part 2 | Theophilus' Doctrine of Scripture

considerably more success with later Christians, who transformed the Sibyl into a prophetess who foretold Christ."[27]

References to the Sibyl appear in various Christian authors of the second century and beyond, such as Justin,[28] Athenagoras,[29] Clement of Alexandria,[30] Tertullian,[31] and Augustine,[32] but most prominently in Lactantius.[33] The Sibyl even famously made her way to the ceiling of the Sistine chapel painted by Michelangelo.

Likewise, Jane Lightfoot describes the general understanding of the early Jews and Christians in these words, "The Sibyl is an inspired prophet. It is a god who impels her; the inspiration does not come from within, but from without."[34] Though the Sibyl was common in other second and third-century writers it was in no way unanimous; however, some have seen Theophilus' use of the Sibyl as more weighty than other early writers. As Rogers points out, "While the inclusion of the Sibyl among the authentic prophets has become apologetic convention in the second century, Theophilus' is more vigorous than most."[35] Harnack even argues that Theophilus viewed the Sibyl as of equal authority to that of the Old Testament.[36] Grant says that she is Theophilus' "favorite poetess, or rather prophetess."[37] Even

---

27. Collins, *Apocalypse, Prophecy, and Pseudepigraphy*, 267.

28. Justin Martyr, *First Apology* 20, 44. Ciholas has said that "the earliest extensive quotations of Sibylline oracles among the church fathers appeared in Justin;" Ciholas, *The Omphalos and the Cross*, 152. See Ciholas, *The Emphalos and the Cross*, 152–169 for a fuller treatment of how the Sibyl appears in the Christian literature of the second and third centuries.

29. Athenagoras, *Plea for Christians*, 30.

30. Clement of Alexandria, *Exhortation to the Heathen*; *Paedagogus* 3.3; and *Stromata*.

31. Tertullian, *Ad Nationes* II.12.

32. Augustine, *City of God* 18.23–4, 46.

33. Lactantius, *Divine Institutes, Epitome*. Cf. Parke, "The Sibyl in Christian Literature" 152–73.

34. Lightfoot, *Sibylline Oracles*, 8.

35. Rogers, *Theophilus of Antioch*, 136.

36. Von Harnack, *Das Neue Testament um das Jahr 200: Theodor Zahn's Geschichte des neutestamentlichen Kanons*, 39–40. Cf. Hooker, "The Use of Sibyls and Sibylline Oracles in Early Christian Writings," 174. Grant likewise affirms, "Not all Theophilus' information about the past comes from the 'prophets' of the Old Testament. Some of it is confirmed by the Sibylline Oracles, from which he gives three quotations (II 3,31, 36). The Sibyl herself, unlike Greek poets and philosophers, was inspired by God *in the same way* as the prophets (II 9). Theophilus can even speak of 'The Sibyl and the rest of the prophets' (II 38);" Grant, "Theophilus of Antioch to Autolycus," 241.

37. Grant, "The Problem of Theophilus," 181.

Parsons has said that Theophilus "used New Testament literature, along with the Christianized *Sibyllines* as if they possessed theological and religious authority equal to that of the Old Testament."[38] Though the thesis of this book is not overthrown by Theophilus' use of the Sibyl, it does provide an interesting case study in the difficulty of finding a single agreed-upon canon list in the second-century. It also opens the discussion over how broad his category of inspiration was.

There are several reasons why the Sibylline oracles may have appeared so frequently in Theophilus and other Christian writers. Four reasons that stand out are (1) a genuine confusion about their origin; (2) flowing from that, they then provided great polemical and rhetorical weight; (3) a similar apologetic purpose;[39] (4) and those familiar with Scriptures would have seen many biblical allusions and motifs that provide the basis for what we now know as the Jewish and Christian adaptations of the Sybil. For these reasons, the Sibyl often served an important apologetic role in showing how God was active showing the truth even through "one of their own." As Hill points out,

> An instructive test case is the Sibyl. The collection of Sibylline oracles that has survived from antiquity is a fictitious and apologetically motivated Jewish production, which has been further interpolated and supplemented by one or more Christian hands. This seems plain to modern students, but was not so plain to all early Christian writers. Nor, for that matter, was it clear to many Christians living much later, such as Michelangelo, who depicted the four main Sibyls on the Sistine Chapel ceiling along with the Hebrew prophets. Clearly, some Christian writers did not know quite what to do with the Sibyl. For who could, or would want to, deny that she spoke beforehand of the coming of Christ, much like the Hebrew prophets? As perplexing as her "inspiration" might be to us, we note that she did present early Christians an undeniable apologetic opportunity.[40]

This apologetic purpose is seen in Theophilus as well. Theophilus refers to the Sibyl explicitly only in book 2.[41] Theophilus never has to explain

---

38. Parsons, "By One and the Same Spirit," 252.

39. Parsons, "By One and the Same Spirit," 162–3.

40. Hill, "Truth above All Demonstration," 79.

41. Grant, *Theophilus of Antioch*, II.3, 9, 31, 36, 38. Hooker has identified possible allusions to the Sibyl in book 1, but they are uncertain and could have as easily come from biblical material. Cf. Hooker, "The Use of Sibyls and Sibylline Oracles in Early Christian

PART 2 | THEOPHILUS' DOCTRINE OF SCRIPTURE

who the Sibyl is, but he everywhere presupposes that Autolycus is aware of who she is and her writings. Whether Autolycus's knowledge of the Sibyl comes from their in-person conversations or his own previous study is impossible to determine, though the Sibyl as an office was a part of ancient Roman culture since long before the second century. However, due to this seeming agreed-upon source, the Sibyl provides helpful confirming evidence to back up the truth of Christian Scripture. In light of the rhetorical structure and the battle of literature that is being waged in AA, it is fitting that Theophilus would appeal to this source that seems to be recognized also by his opponent.[42]

This appears to be the case for the first occurrence of the Sibyl in II.3 where she is cited as giving evidence of a Greek who spoke of the foolishness of the opinion that the gods were active in procreation. In contrast to this opinion, she affirms that there is only one God that is the creator of all things. Here, there is no explicit explanation of the authority or nature of the Sibyl. Theophilus cites an unknown fragment and makes an allusion to *Oracle* 9.108. For Theophilus, even the Sibyl spoke to the Greeks of the foolishness of their practices and beliefs, yet they still continued in them.

If it is true, as it appears to be, that Autolycus and Theophilus shared a common appreciation for the Sibyl, it must have been because, as Hill mentioned above, they did not see through the pseudepigraphal nature. Theophilus seems to have really believed that the writings he knew as from the Sibyl (citing Oracles 3, 8, 9, and some unknown fragments), were from the Greek Sibyl—a prophetess among the Greeks.[43] He may have even thought that she really was the daughter-in-law of Noah, though he does not mention this affirmation.

Though it is beyond the scope of this book to show the general use and opinion of pseudepigraphal writings that claimed the name Christian in the early church, it is interesting to see that there was great aversion in some Christian writers to *known* forgeries.[44] The most notable evidence of this,

---

Writings," 164.

42. In light of this apparent shared appreciation, Dillon says, concerning Theophilus' use of the Sibyl, that "I trust [it] impressed Autolycus;" Dillon, "Review of *Theophilus of Antioch, Ad Autolycum* by Robert M. Grant," 88.

43. Grant, *Theophilus of Antioch*, II.9.

44. Kruger points out several helpful arguments to demonstrate this, including several contemporaries of Theophilus—such as Tertullian and the Muratorian Canon—and even Paul himself in 2 Thessalonians 2:2, 3:17; Kruger, "The Authenticity of 2 Peter," 647–9. Metzger also provides other arguments for a patristic aversion to pseudepigraphal

which is very insightful in a study of Theophilus, is an affirmation by Serapion of Antioch, who was the second to hold the bishopric after Theophilus. According to Eusebius, he wrote a book *Concerning What is Known as the Gospel of Peter* where he says, "For our part, brethren, we receive both Peter and the other apostles as Christ, but the writings which falsely bear their names we reject, as men of experience, knowing that *such were not handed down to us*."[45] Serapion himself seems to indicate that this was the custom that he had received, maybe even indirectly through Theophilus. Due to this attitude toward pseudepigraphal writings that was present in Antioch at least a few years after Theophilus, if not during his time, it therefore appears to be the case that Theophilus could make use of the Sibyl because he genuinely believed her oracles to be from whom they claim to be.

The most obvious thing that Theophilus believes about the Sibyl is that she is absolutely unique among the Greeks. As Hooker has said, "[T]he Sibyl is in fact the *only* figure from Greek culture who can rightly be called an analogue of the Hebrew prophets, despite the fact that Greek philosophers and poets did sometimes speak truth."[46] In II.9 he says, "There were not just one or two of them [prophets] but more at various times and seasons among the Hebrews, as well as the Sibyl among the Greeks."[47] Though there was a multitude of prophets among the Hebrews, he seems to recognize that the Sibyl was the only source of *consistent* truth among the Greeks. This passage also demonstrates how he really believed that the writings he cites were from the Greek Sibyl. However, the most challenging thing about this passage is the close parallel that he makes between the Sibyl and the scriptural prophets, which will be addressed shortly.

According to II.31, the Sibyl was also a source for Theophilus' understanding of ancient history, and he uses a combined citation from parts of *Oracle* 3 and 8 to confirm the scriptural testimony about the Tower of Babel. In this passage, there is no explicit reference to inspiration, but it is interestingly fitted into a long list of references to the book of Genesis.

---

writings in his article, Metzger, "Literary Forgeries and Canonical Pseudepigrapha" 3–24.

45. Eusebius, *Ecclesiastical History*, 6.12.1.

46. Hooker, "The Use of Sibyls and Sibylline Oracles in Early Christian Writings," 173–4. "[I]t is possible or even likely, but not certain, that Sibylline texts influenced Theophilus more than appears from Book 2 of the *Ad Autolycum*;" Hooker, "The Use of Sibyls and Sibylline Oracles in Early Christian Writings," 164. The intertextual nature of the Jewish and Christian sibylline oracles, especially their use of Scripture, makes it rather difficult to identify intentional or unintentional intertextual uses of the Sibyls.

47. Grant, *Theophilus of Antioch*, II.9.

PART 2 | THEOPHILUS' DOCTRINE OF SCRIPTURE

This chapter is unlike the scriptural-saturated arguments mentioned above, though it is similar. If it were one, that would be a pretty convincing argument for her authority. However, this passage is a presentation of post-flood history through the lens of Genesis 10–14. The insertion of a single quote to the Sibyl here seems to merely serve as a confirmatory witness to the primary witness of Scripture. Since his main source is Scripture, particularly Genesis, it would be difficult to argue from this passage that the Sibyl has equal authority to that of Scripture, though she did obviously speak things consistent with Scripture about ancient history. For this reason, he can appeal to her as a confirmation of scriptural testimony. It is the Sibyl's similarity and consistency with Scripture that fuels his appreciation for her and not the other way around. Theophilus' main conviction appears to be the authority of Scripture, but sees in the Sibyl a faithful, prophetic witness to the truth of Scripture among the Greeks.

II.36 is a whole chapter dedicated to confirmatory affirmations from the Sibyl about the things taught in Scripture concerning God and creation. This chapter has two lengthy citations from fragment 1 and fragment 3. He begins this chapter by saying, "And the Sibyl, who was a prophetess for the Greeks and the other nations, rebukes the human race at the beginning of her prophecy."[48] The idea of prophet in Theophilus is often connected to the idea of divine inspiration. However, it is so often *explicitly* connected with divine inspiration that it may be significant that he does not use the same attribution of divine inspiration here. He concludes two extensive quotes from the Sibyl with the statement, "Now that these statements are true and useful and just and lovely is obvious to all men."[49] This passage appears to be an allusion to Philippians 4:8, but the use of the allusion does not require that Theophilus had intended an equation of the Sibyl with Scripture. Rather, it is interesting to see how he is using Paul's criteria to judge the value of these fragments from the Sibyl, and thus their usefulness to be read by Christians, which is not to equate them with Scripture. From this affirmation it is possible to affirm that for Theophilus the Scriptures, including the New Testament, had a greater authority than the Sibyl.[50]

In fact, part of what appealed most to Theophilus and other Christian writers was the abundant parallels between the Sibylline oracles and

---

48. Grant, *Theophilus of Antioch*, II.36.
49. Grant, *Theophilus of Antioch*, II.36.
50. Cf. Parsons, "By One and the Same Spirit," 252, where he seems to put the New Testament and the Sibyl on the same level in Theophilus.

Theophilus' Use of Non-Canonical Writings

the Scriptures. As Lightfoot points out, "I submit that her use of Scripture, which is not to be minimized, has its context in expectations about prophecy that were moulded by biblical patterns and paradigms."[51] This appears to be what attracted Theophilus to these two quotes included in his work. These two citations are full of affirmations of the oneness of God, that he is the creator of all things who governs all things in his providence. And, then, on the basis of this reality, she calls all men to turn from the vain worship of idols to the true worship of the one God. For example, fragment 1 concludes saying, "Know this, setting wisdom in your hearts: there is one God, who sends rains, winds, earthquakes, lightnings, famines, plagues, and baneful griefs, and snow and ice. Why should I tell forth each one? He guides the heaven, rules the earth, himself exists."[52] This text echoes the same affirmations made elsewhere in Theophilus about the incomprehensibility of God, the sole monarchy of God, and the fact that God created and governs all things and judges all men, which he derives from the consistent witness of Scripture.

He then cites fragment 3 to condemn the opinion of the Greeks on the existence of "created gods." This text echoes the biblical language of creation from Genesis 1 and even speaks of man being set as the ruler over all the different creatures (Gen 1:26–28). The reality of the one Creator God and man as the ruler of all creatures serves to demonstrate the utter folly of idol worship whereby the man set as ruler over creation becomes subservient to creation and makes the created thing to be his god (cf. Rom 1:21–23). For this reason, all those who seek him truly can expect the recompense of righteousness, while all those who continue in folly and idolatry will be judged. These two most lengthy citations give support for Lightfoot's argument and show that Theophilus appreciated the Sibyl precisely because of the many echoes of scriptural truth that he read in her oracles. So, as the allusion to Philippians 4:8 indicates at the end of these citations, it appears that Theophilus recognizes the value of these writings because he sees and hears in her exactly what Scripture had taught him to admire. Scripture speaks these same truths and calls believers to dedicate their thinking to things that are true, useful, just, and lovely, and this is precisely what he finds in the Sibyl.

If one compares the placement of these quotes of the Sibyl in II.36 with the quote and allusion in II.3, it is interesting to note how the structure

---

51. Lightfoot, *Sibylline Oracles,* 242.
52. Grant, *Theophilus of Antioch,* II.36.

Part 2 | Theophilus' Doctrine of Scripture

seems to indicate a secondary authority to the Sibyl when compared to the Law, Prophets, and Gospel. As indicated above, book 2 begins with a critique of pagan philosophy and poetry.[53] The appearance of the Sibyl in this section is very fitting to show the greater darkness of the Greek poets and philosophers as they were so far from the truth that can be found in the oracles of the Sibyl. The bright light shining in the Sibyl's oracles make the folly of the philosophers and poets seem so much darker. For Theophilus, they do not make these errors in the absence of light, but having received the truth through the Sibyl they still continued in their errors. However, the positive defense of his own worldview spans from chapter 10 to 35, being bracketed by Scripture-saturated arguments and centered around scriptural exegesis. Book 2, chapters 36–38 return to Greek literature and focus on the Sibyl and how she agreed with the Scriptures along with the occasional poet or prophet who agreed with Scripture, though in their case often unwillingly. The Sibyl was unique among the Greeks. He even makes this part of his argument clear in II.38 where he says, "Therefore the Sibyl and the other prophets, as well as the poets and philosophers themselves, also spoke about justice and judgement and punishment, and furthermore about providence."[54] In this way the Sibyl is not used in the main body of his argument, except for in the brief confirmatory argument of II.31 by which he confirms the biblical account of the Tower of Babel. The comparison of the role of Scripture and the Sibyl in his rhetorical structure helps to clarify her secondary and corroborating authority.

A counterargument to this presentation of Theophilus' approach to the Sibyl is her appearance in the key fulcrum passage of II.9. This is indeed a difficult passage where Theophilus appears to put the Sibyl in the same category as the other prophets. As a rebuttal to that, it is interesting to compare the descriptions of the scriptural prophets and that of the Sibyl in the other books. In I.14 he refers to "the sacred writings of the holy prophets, who [prophesied] through the Spirit of God . . ."[55] In II.10 the scriptural prophets are explicitly connected to divine inspiration, as well as in II.30 where Moses and the prophets are mentioned, which naturally and contextually is a reference to the Old Testament. The scriptural prophets are also explicitly connected to divine inspiration in II.33. Divine inspiration and consistency are applied to the scriptural prophets in his Scripture-saturated

---

53. Grant, *Theophilus of Antioch*, II.2–8.
54. Grant, *Theophilus of Antioch*, II.38.
55. Grant, *Theophilus of Antioch*, I.14.

Theophilus' Use of Non-Canonical Writings

argument found in II.35. However, when he arrives to II.36 and his use of the Sibyl, he merely says, "the Sibyl, who was a prophetess among the Greeks and the other nations . . ."[56] One cannot be dogmatic, but it seems to be significant that the scriptural prophets are regularly connected with the attributes of Scripture mentioned above, but the Sibyl, when it comes to her main role in the apology, does not receive such appellations.

Therefore, it appears that the Sibyl's authority, for Theophilus, is not absolute and independent of Scripture, rather she is cited in order to confirm Scripture, not as one and the same with Scripture. Though including her in II.9 seems to blur the lines and opens the door for a broader concept of inspiration, her actual usage in II.36 serves to show the confirmatory nature of her authority. This is also confirmed by how she does not appear in book 3 where he affirms the unity and consistency of Scripture in III.12, 17, 18, 23.[57] If his intention in II.9 was to truly classify the Sibyl as fully equal to the Old Testament prophets, it is interesting to note that he does not confirm that status in the rest of his work. It is obvious that she is equal in some respect, speaking God's truth with the aid of the Spirit among the Greeks and being consistent with Scripture, but the evidence does not appear to fully support the affirmations of Harnack and others.

Second, he recognizes the value of the Sibyl[58] but he never inculcates diligent study of her oracles as he does the Scriptures.[59] Also, it is thanks to the Law and prophets, a reference to the Old Testament Scripture, that the world is not consumed.[60] A clear example of this that shows the confirmatory nature of the Sibyl along with all other sources is in II.34, where he says, "Furthermore, you must devotedly search the things of God [what things? And where do we find them?], I mean those spoken through the prophets, so that by comparing what is said by us with what is said by the others you will be able to discover the truth."[61] He later explains this more fully by referring to the "law and . . . holy prophets" in conjunction with allusions to First Peter and Acts. The Sibyl is not found in this context,

---

56. Grant, *Theophilus of Antioch*, II.36.

57. In some of these places cited in this paragraph, it may possibly be argued that he always included the Sibyl in his category of "prophet," however, this is unlikely. In the context it is often connected to scriptural/canonical prophets, and many times the Sibyl is distinguished from "the other prophets." Cf. Grant, *Theophilus of Antioch*, II.35, 38.

58. Grant, *Theophilus of Antioch*, II.36.

59. Grant, *Theophilus of Antioch*, I.14, II.30, 34, 35.

60. Grant, *Theophilus of Antioch*, II.14.

61. Grant, *Theophilus of Antioch*, II.34.

rather she enters the discussion in II.36. Therefore, he does not include himself or any other source in the same category as the "things of God." However, their truth, though flowing from the fact of their inspiration, can be confirmed and illuminated by Theophilus' own teaching ("a living voice"),[62] the Sibyl,[63] and the occasional grain of truth in the poets and philosophers.[64] This also serves to demonstrate the important rhetorical placement of the main references to the Sibyl in II.36.

One may seek to argue further from the fact that the New Testament writers do not even appear in II.9, that key passage which *does* mention the Sibyl. However, in III.12 he not only shows statements that confirm the Christian ethic revealed in the Law, in the prophets and Gospels,[65] (something argued from the Sibyl in II.36, 38), but he explicitly connects that consistency to this reason: "because all the inspired men made utterances by means of the one Spirit of God."[66] He does not affirm this about the Sibyl in II.36 or 38. Also, the Pauline letters are referred to as the divine word, which is not something said of the Sibyl.[67]

Being a prophetess, the Sibyl is consistent with the truth in a way that is unique among the Greeks. The Greek poets and prophets sometimes confirm the truth but normally unwillingly, and they often contradict those same affirmations in other parts of their writings. However, the Sibyl is a consistent and helpful (and convenient, apologetical) source of truth among the Greeks since she is truly a prophetess, unlike the false prophets of the Egyptians and Chaldeans.[68] For this reason, though the high praise given to the Sibyl does indicate an idea of inspiration that is broader than just the writings of the Old and New Testament, it does not open the door wide for any book to enter into this category. In fact, according to the evidence we have in Theophilus' affirmations about prophetic inspiration, the only possible exception to inspiration being limited to the prophetic scriptures is the Sibyl. On the basis of this, one cannot argue that since he saw the

---

62. Grant, *Theophilus of Antioch*, II.38.
63. Grant, *Theophilus of Antioch*, II.36.
64. Grant, *Theophilus of Antioch*, II.37.
65. Grant indicates that the references to the Gospels might have been lost in the text's transmission, but he does later use several passages from Matthew to make a similar point. Cf. Grant, *Ad Autolycus*, 117, n.12.1.
66. Grant, *Theophilus of Antioch*, II.12.
67. Grant, *Theophilus of Antioch*, III.14.
68. Grant, *Theophilus of Antioch*, II.33.

Theophilus' Use of Non-Canonical Writings

Sibyl as inspired Theophilus had no canonical consciousness and any book could have been inspired for him. He is so consistent in affirming the divine origin and authority of the scriptural writings that the Sibyl's inspiration stands out as a unique exception in all ancient literature.

One final argument for a secondary place of the Sibyl in Theophilus is the fact that she never appears weaved into his argument as do the Old Testament and New Testament Scriptures. She is never included in one of the key Scripture-saturated arguments that are found in I.6–7, II.10, II.34–35, and III.11–14. These passages which serve to show the consistency of truth and ethic across his whole canon, do not include the Sibyl. Also, his chronology, where he had occasion to refer to the Sibyl's references to the flood and its history, which he does do in II.31, does not use the Sibyl as an argument for the antiquity of Christian literature. Rather, from a wholistic perspective, his understanding of Christian foundational writings seems to only have in mind the Old Testament and New Testament (though most importantly in this section the book of the Law). He sees the long line of prophets from Moses to Zechariah as the center of the Christian's claim to antiquity, without reference to the Sibyl.[69]

Therefore, in conclusion, in book 2, Theophilus definitely has a great appreciation for the Sibylline oracles. They are unique among the Greeks and are consistent with the Scriptures and are the product of a prophetess. However, due to the foundational authority that he sees in Scripture consistently throughout the whole work, and the seeming peripheral role that the Sibyl plays rhetorically, it can be concluded that it does not fit the evidence for Harnack and others to affirm that he held the Sibyl to be on the same level and with the same authority as Scripture nor for the claim that he had no limited view of inspiration. If we think of this authority in terms

---

69. Cf. Grant, *Theophilus of Antioch*, III.23. An interesting speculation is that if Grant (*Greek Apologists*, 143–4) is right about several years separating book 2 and 3, maybe the silence of book 3 on the Sibyl, especially when it might have been convenient in confirming ancient history and showing the antiquity of Christianity (cf. II.29, where he uses the corroborating evidence of a Chaldean historian, and even refers to the events like the flood which he mentions from the Sibyl in II.31), was due to a realization of its pseudepigraphal nature in those intervening years. The silence is even more interesting in light of III.30 where he says, "the Greeks make no mention of the histories which give the truth . . ." This is unproveable due to a lack of a clear retraction (though it may have happened in their in-person correspondence) especially since he does refer to Book II at times. This does serve to set forth the possibility that Celsus's critique of the Christians for their use of the Sibyl, which he saw as forged and interpolated by Christians, might have "hit home" with Theophilus (cf. Origen, *Contra Celsum*, 7.53, 56). Hooker, "The Use of the Sibyl and Sibylline Oracles," 174–5.

of being the authoritative divine rule for faith and life, it is the Scriptures of the Old and New Testament that are consistently and exclusively used in this way in Theophilus.

CONCLUSION

We have seen in Theophilus that the Scriptures play a key role. With respect to the Law, Prophets, Gospels, and Epistles, Theophilus both (1) makes explicit affirmations about their divine and authoritative nature and (2) uses them extensively to undergird the structure and content of his argument. On the other hand, his use of Christian and Apocryphal works does not include explicit affirmations of their divine nature and even some allusions attributed to them may actually be allusions to the canonical Scriptures or be the result of a shared cognitive environment. The fact that they are at times weaved into the structure of the argument along with New Testament and Old Testament allusions is significant, however, since it has been shown how scriptural allusions play such an important role in his argument.[70] However, this reality emphasizes the difficulty of defining the clear limits of Theophilus' canon and does not change in any way what we have seen to be his understanding of the nature of that canon.

The Sibyl on the other hand, does not appear in allusions and echoes all throughout the work as the New Testament, Old Testament and occasional apocryphal reference do, and it seems to mainly be relegated to a secondary and supporting role in his argument. However, unlike the apocryphal works, the Sibyl is more closely linked with the work of the Spirit that is found in the scriptural prophets in some of his explicit affirmations. But, Scripture, Old Testament and New Testament (with their exact contents still being "fuzzy"), are both intimately weaved into the structure of his argument and are regularly explicitly mentioned as divine, inspired, authoritative, and perfectly consistent in every way. Only Scripture consistently and repeatedly meets both criteria.

---

70. Parsons, *Ancient Apologetic Exegesis*.

Conclusion

ANY CLASSICAL WORK OF ancient rhetoric was expected to end with a *recapitulation*. Therefore, this work likewise will conclude by recapitulating and summarizing the arguments that have been made. This book began by seeing Theophilus in the broader context of the second century and then giving an introduction to his life and works. Then, it gave a brief introduction to the current trends in scholarship on Theophilus, especially with respect to his understanding of Christ, the Trinity, and Scripture. Chapter 3 presented a more general understanding of the worldview apologetic that Theophilus uses in AA. Chapter 4 then begins the main argument of this book by looking at his understanding of the Bible and its role in his apology. Chapters 5 to 8 then presented a positive case for his understanding of the necessity, authority, inspiration, antiquity, and consistency of Scripture. Each of these points were first seen in Theophilus and then confirmed by appeal to other writers of the second century. Finally, chapter 9 looked at Theophilus' use of non-canonical works, specifically the Sibyl.

From what we can know about Theophilus and his view of Scripture, it appears evident that he did truly have a *high view* of Scripture. Scripture, for him, is the basis of his worldview—his understanding of God, the world, creation, man, judgment, and the Christian life. This book has sought to give a systematic presentation of what Theophilus thought about Scripture as gleaned from what he says in AA. Since only one of his books is extant, which is written in a protreptic style, this book cannot claim to be an exhaustive presentation of his thoughts on Scripture. However, because of his explicit affirmations about the necessity of divine revelation and the authority, inspiration, antiquity, and consistency of Scripture, and the

Conclusion

way Scripture is intimately weaved into his argument, it is clear that Scripture—Old Testament and New Testament—is foundational to his thinking. Though he occasionally alluded to non-canonical works, and he also deeply appreciated the Sibyl, it has been shown that they do not have the same foundational role as the canonical Scriptures.

As he defended Christianity, Theophilus put Scripture at the very center of his argument, both metaphorically and literally. He saturated his defense of the biblical faith with an abundance of scriptural citations and allusions, and he even dedicated a major part of his argument to an interpretation of Genesis 1–11. For Theophilus, the Scriptures are necessary for the Christian and the world, and they are an authoritative rule and guide for faith and life that is inspired by the one Spirit of God and therefore the most consistent and trustworthy source of truth. His argument was full of Scripture so that, as he himself was converted by reading them, his friend Autolycus too would believe in God and receive his grace by diligent and humble study of the truths of Scripture. The Scriptures were the "power of God" unto his own salvation (Rom 1:16), and he hoped that it would have that same effect in Autolycus. Autolycus was already a lover of learning, but Theophilus hoped he would become a genuine lover of truth. Though we do not know the final result of this correspondence in the life of Autolycus, Scripture is able to make one wise for salvation through faith (2 Tim 3:15), as evidenced in Theophilus himself. His apologetic for the Christian faith demonstrates this conviction throughout as he holds forth the divine words of the Law, Prophets, Gospels, and Epistles as the "counsellor and pledge of the truth."[1]

In this way, this book has presented the Scripture-saturated apologetic of Theophilus of Antioch and has sought to shed light on the doctrine of Scripture in the second century. I hope this book will serve to foster a greater appreciation for the much-neglected Theophilus, and that others will take up the important task of giving thorough treatments of the status of Scripture and nature of inspiration in other early church fathers.

---

1. Grant, *Theophilus of Antioch*, III.30.

Appendix 1

Theophilus' Use of Scripture

This list has been reproduced from Grant, *Theophilus of Antioch*, 149–50. However, it has also been supplemented with results from BiblIndex online database for patristic citations and allusions for Scripture: http://www.biblindex.mom.fr/citation_biblique/?lang=en. Verses marked with (*) are citations, while others are allusions.

ORGANIZED BY BIBLICAL BOOK

Old Testament

Genesis

1:1–2	II.10*, II.13
1:3–2:3	II.11*
2:4–7	II.19*
2:8–3:19	II.20–21*
4:1–2	II.29*
4:9–14	II.29*
4:17–22	II.30*
7:11–12	III.19
7:20	III.19
9:1	II.32
9:11	III.9
10:5	II.32
10:10–14	II.31
11:1, 4, 7	II.31
11:31	II.31
14:1–6	II.31
14:18	II.31
15:13	III.10
20:2	II.31
23:10	II.31
26:1	II.31

Exodus

1:11	III.20
4:11	I.14
12:40	III.10
20:3–5	III.9*
20:7	II.10
20:12–17	III.9*
20:13–17	II.35
23:6–8	III.9*
23:9	III.10*

Appendix 1

Deuteronomy
  4:19   II.35
  18:15   III.11

2 Kings
  15:29   II.31
  17:3   II.31
  18:13   II.31

Job
  9:8   I.7
  9:9   I.6
  12:15   I.6
  34:14–15   I.7
  37:15   I.6
  38:10   I.6
  38:18   I.7
  38:22   I.6
  38:31   I.6
  38:35   I.6

Psalms (LXX)
  13:1, 3   II.35*
  23:2   I.7
  32:6   I.7
  32:7   I.6
  44:2   II.10
  50:10   II.38*
  54:20   II.10
  64:8   I.7
  88:10   I.7
  93:9   I.14
  94:4   I.4
  95:5   I.10
  103:5   I.4
  103:14   I.4
  109:3   II.10
  113:9   I.14
  113:12–14   I.1 I.10 II.34
  113:16   I.10
  134:7   I.6
  134:15   I.10, II.34
  134:18   I.10
  146:4   I.6
  146:8   I.4

Proverbs
  3:8   II.38
  3:19–20   I.7
  4:25   II.35*
  4:25–6   III.13*
  6:27–9   III.13*
  8:22   II.10
  8:27–9   II.10*
  24:21–2   I.11*

Ecclesiastes
  11:7   I.6

Isaiah
  1:16–17   III.12*
  11:6–9   II.17
  30:27, 30, 28   II.38*
  31:6   III.11*
  40:22   II.13*
  40:28   II.35*
  42:5–6   II.35*
  43:25   III.12
  45:3   I.6
  45:12   II.35*
  45:22   III.11*
  55:6–7   III.11*
  58:6–8   III.11
  60:21   II.15
  66:1   I.4, II.22
  66:5   III.14*

Jeremiah
  6:9   III.11*
  6:16   III.12*
  6:22   III.25
  6:29   II.35*
  9:23   III.12

10:12–13	I.6, II.35*	16:31	I.8
10:14–15	II.35*	18:27	II.13
16:15	III.25	John	
28:15–16	II.35	1:1–3	II.22*
Ezekiel		1:3	II.10
18:21–3	II.17, III.11*	12:24	I.13
Hosea		14:26	III.11
12:7	III.12*	15:26	II.38
13:4	II.35* III.12*	16:8, 13	II.38, III.15
14:10	II.38*	20:27	I.14
Joel		Acts	
1:14	III.12	15:20, 29	II.34
2:16	III.12*	Romans	
Habakkuk		1:22	II.35
2:18–19	II.35*	1:23	III.30
Zechariah		1:30	I.2
7:9–10	III.12*	2:6–9	I.14
9:9	III.12	2:18	I.7
Malachi		5:18–19	II.22
1:9	III.12*	11:33	II.12
3:19 (heb. 4:1)	II.38*	13:1	I.11
		13:1–3	III.14
		13:7–8	III.14*
New Testament		First Corinthians	
Matthew		1:18	III.4
3:15	III.19	1:24	II.22
4:23	III.21	2:9	I.14
5:8	I.2	2:10	II.34
5:28	III.13*	2:18	II.35
5:32	III.13*	3:18	II.35
5:44, 46	III.14*	6:8–10	I.2
6:3	III.14*	6:9–10	I.14
13:32	II.14	8:4	II.1
19:17, 25	II.27	9:17	I.11
25:46	2.34	9:26	III.1
Luke		12:11	I.13, II.35
1:2–3	III.2	15:50	II.27
1:35	II.10	15:53–4	I.7

Appendix 1

Second Corinthians
- 7:1 — I.2
- 11:6 — II.1
- 11:19 — III.4

Galatians
- 4:19 — II.35
- 5:22 — I.14

Ephesians
- 1:19 — I.3, II.12
- 3:10 — I.6, II.16

Philippians
- 1:10 — I.2
- 3:19 — II.17
- 4:8 — II.36

Colossians
- 1:15 — II.22
- 1:16 — II.10
- 3:2 — II.17

First Thessalonians
- 4:8 — II.15

First Timothy
- 1:10 — I.2
- 2:1–2 — I.11, III.14

Second Timothy
- 3:2 — I.2
- 3:8 — I.1

Titus
- 1:7 — I.2
- 3:1 — III.14*
- 3:5 — II.16

Philemon
- 1:11 — I.1

Hebrews
- 5:12 — II.25
- 11:35 — II.27

First Peter
- 1:18 — II.34
- 2:15, 17 — I.11
- 3:20 — III.19
- 4:3 — I.14, II.34

Second Peter
- 1:21 — II.9

Revelation
- 12:9 — II.14

THEOPHILUS' USE OF SCRIPTURE

ORGANIZED BY AA PLACEMENT

Book I		Ch. 10	Ps 113:12; 134:15
Ch. 1	2 Tim 3:8		Ps 95:5
	Ps. 113:12–14		Ps 113:16; 134:18
	Phil 1:11	Ch. 11	Rom 13:1
Ch. 2	Rom 2:18		1 Cor 9:17
	Phil 1:10		1 Pet 2:17
	2 Cor 7:1		1 Tim 2:2
Ch. 4	Ps 103:5		1 Pet 2:15
	Ps 94:4		Prov 24:21
	Isa 66:1	Ch. 13	Luke 16:31
	Gen 1:14		John 12:24
	Ps 103:14; 146:8		1 Cor 12:11
Ch. 6	Job 38:31	Ch. 14	John 20:27
	Job 9:9		Ex 4:11; Ps 93:9
	Eph 3:10		Rom 2:6–7
	Ps 146:4		1 Cor 2:9
	Job 37:15		Rom 2:8
	Job 9:9		1 Pet 4:3
	Ps 32:7		Rom 2:8
	Job 38:10		
	Job 38:22	**Book II**	
	Isa 45:3		
	Ecc 11:7	Ch. 1	2 Cor 11:6
	Jer 10:13	Ch. 2	1 Cor 8:4
	Ps 134:7	Ch. 10	Ps 54:20
	Job 38:35		Ps 109:3
	Job 21:15		Ps 44:2
Ch. 7	Job 9:8		John 1:3
	Job 38:18		Gen 1:2
	Ps 64:8		Gen 1:1
	Ps 23:2		Prov 8:22
	Gen 1:2		Luke 1:35
	Job 34:14		Prov 8:27–9
	Ps 32:6		Gen 1:1
	Prov 3:19		Exod 20:7
	1 Cor 15:53		Col 1:16

Appendix 1

	Gen 1:1–2		Rom 5:18–19
Ch. 11	Gen 1:3–2:3		Matt 19:25
Ch. 12	Eph 1:19		Heb 11:35
	Rom 11:33		1 Cor 15:50
Ch. 13	Luke 18:27	Ch. 28	Gen 3:5
	Gen 1:1		Gen 2:23–24
	Gen 1:3		Rev 12:9
	Isa 40:22	Ch. 29	Gen 4:1–2
	Gen 1:3		Gen 4:9
Ch. 14	Matt 13:32		Gen 4:9–14
Ch. 15	1 Thes 4:8	Ch. 30	Gen 4:17
	Isa 60:21		Gen 4:18–22
Ch. 16	Eph 3:10	Ch. 31	Gen 10:10–14
	Tit 3:5		Gen 11:1
Ch. 17	Phil 3:19		Gen 11:4
	Ezk 18:21–3		Gen 11:7
	Col 3:2		Gen 11:31
	Gen 1:31		Gen 14:1
	Isa. 11:6–9		Gen 14:2
Ch. 18	Gen 1:26		Gen 14:4
Ch. 19	Gen. 2:4–5		Gen 14:5–6
	Gen 2:6–7		Gen 14:18
Ch. 20	Gen 2:8–2:25		Gen 20:2
Ch. 21	Gen 3:1–19		Gen 26:1
Ch. 22	Isa 66:1		Gen 23:10
	1 Cor 1:24		2 Kgs 15:29
	Col 1:15		2 Kgs 17:3
	John 1:1		2 Kgs 18:13
	John 1:1–3		Gen 9:1
Ch. 23	Gen 3:16		Gen 10:5
	Gen 1:28	Ch. 34	1 Cor 2:10
	Gen 3:14		Ps 113:12
Ch. 24	Gen 2:8–9		1 Pet 4:3
	Gen 2:15–16		Acts 15:20, 29
Ch. 25	Heb 5:12	Ch. 35	Deut 4:19
Ch. 26	Gen. 2: 8, 15		Ex 20:13–17
	Gen 3:9		Prov 4:25
Ch. 27	Matt 19:17		Hos 13:4

Theophilus' Use of Scripture

	Isa 42:5–6		Jer 6:9
	Isa 45:12	Ch. 12	Isa 1:16–17
	Isa 40:28		Isa 58:6–8
	Jer 10:12–13		Jer 6:16
	1 Cor 12:11		Zech 9:9
	Gal 4:19		Jer 9:23
	Rom 1:22		Hos 12:7, 13:4
	Jer 10:14–15		Joel 2:16
	Ps 13:1, 3		Joel 1:14
	Hab 2:18–19		Isa 43:25
Ch. 38	Mal 3:19		Zech 7:9–10
	Isa 30:27,30,28	Ch. 13	Prov 4:25
	John 16:8		Mat 5:28
	John 16:13		Matt 5:32
	Prov 3:8		Prov 6:27–29
	Ps 50:10	Ch. 14	Isa 66:15
	Hos 14:9–10		Matt 5:44, 46
			Matt 6:3
			Rom 13:1–3
Book III			1 Tim 2:1–2
			Rom 13:7–8
Ch. 2	Luke 1:2–3		Gen 9:11
	1 Cor 9:26	Ch. 19	1 Pet 3:20
Ch. 4	2 Cor 11:19		Gen 7:11
	1 Cor 1:18		Gen 7:20
Ch. 9	Ex 20:3–5		Ex 1:11
	Ex 20:12	Ch. 20	Matt 4:23
	Ex 20:13–17	Ch. 21	Jer 6:22; 16:15
	Ex 23:6–8	Ch. 25	Rom 1:23
	Matt 3:15	Ch. 30	
Ch. 10	Gen 15:13		
	Ex 12:40		
	Ex 23:9		
Ch. 11	Deut 18:15		
	John 14:26		
	Isa 55:6–7		
	Ezk 18:21–23		
	Isa 31:6		
	Isa 45:22		

APPENDIX 1

CHRISTIAN AND JEWISH NON-CANONICAL REFERENCES

Epistle of Barnabas[1]
    1:7   I.14
    5:10   I.5
    10   II.16

Baruch
    2:4   III.11

Epistle to Diognetus[2]
    7   II.8

First Esdras
    2:32   III.29

Second Esdras
    1:8   III.25

Justin's *First Apology*
    I.4.9   III.30

Second Maccabees
    7:28   1.4

First Clement
    14:3   II.14

Kerygma Petri
    fr. 3   I.14

Sibyl[3]
    iii. 97–103, 105   II.31*
    viii. 5   II.31*
    ix. 108   II.3
    fr. 1   II.36*
    fr. 2   II.3*
    fr. 3   II.36*

---

1. Proposed by Ferguson, "*Theophilus of Antioch*," 112.
2. Also proposed by Ferguson, "*Theophilus of Antioch*," 112.
3. Charlesworth, *The Old Testament Pseudepigrapha*. Cf. Geffcken, ed. "*Die Oracula Sibyllina*," 8:1–226.

Appendix 2

Outline of *Ad Autolycum*

BOOK 1: THE SEARCH FOR TRUTH (*HOMILIA*)

Introduction—ch. 1
How man may really know God—ch. 2–8
    Sin has blinded man—ch. 2
    The nature of God—ch. 3–4
    God is known through natural revelation—ch. 5–6
    Faith necessary to properly know God—ch. 7–8
The absurdities of Pagan idolatry—ch. 9–10
Misconceptions about Christianity corrected—ch. 11–13
    Christians and Imperial Worship—ch. 11
    The name of Christian—ch. 12
    A defense of the resurrection of the body—ch. 13
Theophilus' conversion account—ch. 14

BOOK 2: SUPERIORITY OF CHRISTIANITY IN ITS ACCOUNT OF CREATION (*SYNGRAMMA*)

Introduction—ch. 1
The absurdities of paganism—ch. 2–8
    The absurdities of their idea of God—ch. 2–5
        The vanity of idols—ch. 2–3
        The philosophers' idea of God—ch. 4–5

Appendix 2

    The absurdities of their idea of creation—ch. 6–7
    The absurdities of their idea of providence—ch. 8
The worldview system of Christianity—ch. 9–38
    Its source: divine revelation—ch. 9
    The scriptural idea of Creation—ch. 10–13
        The creator-creature distinction—ch. 10
        The six-day creation account—ch. 11–13
            Citation—ch. 11
            Exaltation—ch. 12
            Explanation—ch. 13
    Illustrations drawn from the creation account—ch. 14–17
        The division of sea and land—ch. 14
        Day Four—ch. 15
        Day Five—ch. 16
        Day Six—ch. 17
    The creation of man and paradise—ch. 18–20
        Man's creation—ch. 18
        Description of paradise—ch. 19–20
    The Fall of Man—ch. 21–22
        Citation—ch. 21
        Explanation of God walking in the Garden—ch. 22
    The Creation account explains the world around us—ch. 23
    Man's creation, duty, and Fall explained—ch. 24–28
        The nature of paradise—ch. 24
        The command and punishment of God—ch. 25–26
        The nature of man—ch. 27
        The creation of Eve—ch. 28
    Post-Fall history—ch. 29–32
        Pre-Flood—ch. 29–30
        Post-Flood—ch. 31–32
    The superiority of God's revelation—ch. 33–35
        Scripture comes from God—ch. 33
        Scripture produces a holy life—ch. 34
        Scriptures are consistent—ch. 35
    Corroborating evidence for the scriptural worldview—ch. 36–38
        Scripture confirmed by the Sibyl—ch. 36
        Scripture confirmed by the Greeks—ch. 37–38

BOOK 3: THE VERACITY AND ANTIQUITY OF CHRISTIANITY (*HYPOMNEMA*)

Introduction—ch. 1
A defense of the veracity of Christianity—ch. 2–15
    The foolishness of non-Christian religions—ch. 2–8
        Their contradictions—ch. 2–3
        The ethical misconceptions of Autolycus—ch. 4
        The immorality of the philosophers—ch. 5–8
    The superiority of the Christian ethic—ch. 9–15
A defense of the antiquity of Christianity—ch. 16–30
    The foolishness of pagan ideas of history—ch. 16
    The Christians have divine revelation—ch. 17
    The foolishness of pagan ideas of the Flood—ch. 18
    The biblical account of the Flood—ch. 19
    The antiquity of Moses—ch. 20–21
    The antiquity of the temple—ch. 22
    The antiquity of the prophets—ch. 23
    A chronology from creation to Theophilus' day—ch. 24–28
    The antiquity of Christianity affirmed—ch. 29
    Sin the source of the Greeks' errors—ch. 30

Bibliography

Ackroyd, P. R. and C.F. Evans. *The Cambridge History of the Bible: From the Beginnings to Jerome*. Volume 1. Cambridge, UK: Cambridge University Press, 1976.
Allert, Craig D. *A High View of Scripture?: The Authority of the Bible and the Formation of the New Testament Canon*. Edited by D. H. Williams. Evangelical Ressourcement. Grand Rapids, MI: Baker Academic, 2007.
———. "What Are We Trying to Conserve? Evangelicalism and Sola Scriptura." *The Evangelical Quarterly* 76.4 (2004) 327–48.
Arndt, William, Frederick W. Danker, Walter Bauer, and F. Wilbur Gingrich. *A Greek-English Lexicon of the New Testament and Other Early Christian Literature*. Chicago, IL: University of Chicago Press, 2000.
Bahnsen, Greg L. *Presuppositional Apologetics: Stated and Defended*. Edited by Joel McDurmon. Powder Springs, GA; Nacogdoches, TX: American Vision; Covenant Media, 2008.
Barrett, Matthew, ed. *Credo: Sola Scriptura (December)*. Credo Magazine, 2016.
———, and R. Albert Mohler Jr. *God's Word Alone—the Authority of Scripture: What the Reformers Taught . . . and Why It Still Matters*. The 5 Solas Series. Grand Rapids, MI: Zondervan, 2016.
Bauer, Walter. *Heresy and Orthodoxy in Earliest Christianity*. 2nd ed. Edited by Robert A. Kraft and Gerhard Krode. Sigler, 1996.
Beale, G. K. *Handbook on the New Testament Use of the Old Testament: Exegesis and Interpretation*. Grand Rapids, MI: Baker Academic, 2012.
Beatrice, Pier Franco. "The "Gospel According to the Hebrews" in the Apostolic Fathers." *Novum Testamentum* 48, no. 2 (2006) 147–95.
Beckwith, Roger. "Intertestamental Judaism, Its Literature and Its Significance." *Themelios* 15, no. 3 (1990) 77–81.
———. *The Old Testament Canon of the New Testament Church and Its Background in Early Judaism*. London: SPCK, 1985.
Behr, John. *Irenaeus of Lyons: Identifying Christianity*. Christian Theology in Context. Oxford: Oxford University Press, 2013.

Bibliography

Bentivegna, J. "A Christianity without Christ by Theophilus of Antioch." Edited by Elizabeth A. Livingstone. *Studia Patristica*, vol 13. Berlin: AkademieVerlag, 1975. pp. 107–30.

Berkhof, Louis. *The History of Christian Doctrines*. Grand Rapids, MI: Eerdmans, 1949.

Bingham, D. Jeffrey. "Senses of Scripture in the Second Century: Irenaeus, Scripture and Noncanonical Christian Texts." *The Journal of Religion*. Vol. 97. No. 1 (January 2017) 26–55.

———. "'We Have the Prophets:' Inspiration and the Prophets in Athenagoras of Athens." *Zeitschrift für Antikes Christentum / Journal of Ancient Christianity*. 20.2. (January, 2016) 211–42.

Boer, Harry R. *A Short History of the Early Church*. Grand Rapids: Eerdmans, 1976.

Bouteneff, Peter C. *Beginnings: Ancient Christian Readings of the Biblical Creation Narratives*. Grand Rapids, MI: Baker Academic, 2008.

Brannan, Rick, tran. *The Apostolic Fathers in English*. Bellingham, WA: Lexham, 2012.

Bruce, F. F. *The Canon of Scripture*. Downers Grove, IL: InterVarsity, 1988.

———. *The Spreading Flame: The Rise and Progress of Christianity from Its First Beginnings to Eighth-Century England*. Nashville, TN: Kingsley, 2017.

Bushur, James G. *Irenaeus of Lyons and the Mosaic of Christ: Preaching Scripture in the Era of Martyrdom*. New York: Routledge, 2017.

Calvin, John. *Institutes of the Christian Religion*. Edited by John T. McNeill. Translated by Ford Lewis Battles. 2 vols. The Library of Christian Classics. Louisville, KY: Westminster John Knox, 2011.

Carter, Craig A. *Interpreting Scripture with the Great Tradition: Recovering the Genius of Premodern Exegesis*. Grand Rapids, MI: Baker Academic, 2018.

Chadwick, Henry. *The Early Church*. Rev. ed. Penguin History of the Church. New York: Penguin, 1993. Kindle ed.

Charlesworth, James H. *The Old Testament Pseudepigrapha*. Vol. 1. New York: Yale University Press, 1983.

———. Lee Martin McDonald, and Blake A. Jurgens, eds. *Sacra Scriptura: How "Non-Canonical" Texts Functioned in Early Judaism and Early Christianity*. Vol. 20. Jewish and Christian Texts in Contexts and Related Studies. London: Bloomsbury, 2014.

Ciholas, Paul. *The Omphalos and the Cross: Pagans and Christians in Search of a Divine Center*. Mercer University Press, 2003.

Collins, John J. *Apocalypse, Prophecy, and Pseudepigraphy: On Jewish Apocalyptic Literature*. Grand Rapids, MI: Eerdmans, 2015.

Compton, Madonna Sophia. "Theophilus of Antioch and Irenaeus on Logos and Sophia: The 'Two Hands of God.'" Accessed Online December 18, 2023. https://www.academia.edu/24464054/Theophilus_of_ Antioch_and_Irenaeus_on_Logos_and_Sophia_the_Two_Hands_of_God_ .

Cowan, Steven B. and Terry L. Wilder, eds. *In Defense of the Bible: A Comprehensive Apologetic for the Authority of Scripture*. Nashville, TN: Broadman & Holman, 2013.

Curry, Carl. "The Theogony of Theophilus." *Vigiliae Christianae* 42, no. 4 (1988) 318–26.

D'Ambrosio, Marcellino. *When the Church Was Young: Voices of the Early Fathers*. Cincinnati, OH: Servant, 2014.

DeMar, Gary, ed. *Pushing the Antithesis: The Apologetic Methodology of Greg L. Bahnsen*. Powder Springs, GA: American Vision, 2007.

Dempster, Stephen. "An 'Extraordinary Fact': Torah And Temple And The Contours Of The Hebrew Canon: Part 2." *Tyndale Bulletin* 48, no. 2 (1997) 191–218.

Bibliography

Dillon, John M. "Review of *Theophilus of Antioch, Ad Autolycum* by Robert M. Grant." *The Classical Journal*, Vol. 70, No. 1 (Oct -Nov 1974) 88–89.

Dockery, David S. *Biblical Interpretation Then and Now: Contemporary Hermeneutics in the Light of the Early Church*. Grand Rapids, MI: Baker Book House, 1992.

Ehrman, Bart D. *Lost Christianities: Christian Scriptures and the Battles over Authentication*. Chantilly, VA: The Teaching Company, 2002.

——— and Michael W. Holmes, eds. *The Text of the New Testament in Contemporary Research: Essays on the Status Quaestionis*. 2nd ed. Leiden: Brill, 2013.

Eusebius, *The Ecclesiastical History: English Translation*. Edited by T. E. Page, E. Capps, W. H. D. Rouse, L. A. Post, and E. H. Warmington. Translated by Kirsopp Lake and J. E. L. Oulton. Volume 1. The Loeb Classical Library. Cambridge, MA: Harvard University Press, 1926–32.

Fairweather, W. "The Greek Apologists of the Second Century." *The Biblical World*, Vol. 26, No. 2 (Aug., 1905) 132–143.

Farrar, Frederic W. *Lives of the Fathers: Sketches of Church History in Biography*. Vol. 1. Edinburgh: Adam and Charles Black, 1889.

Ferguson, *Backgrounds of Early Christianity*, 3rd ed. Grand Rapids, MI: Eerdmans, 2003.

———. *Early Christians Speak, 3rd Ed.: Faith and Life in the First Three Centuries*. 3 vols. Abilene, TX: Leafwood, 2011.

———. *The Early Church at Work and Worship: Ministry, Ordination, Covenant, and Canon*. Vol. 1. Eugene, OR: Cascade, 2013.

———. "*Theophilus of Antioch: Ad Autolycum*. By Robert M. Grant. (Oxford Early Christian Texts). Oxford: Clarendon, 1970." *Church History* 41, no. 1 (1972) 112.

Forrest, Benjamin K., Joshua D. Chatraw, and Alister E. McGrath, eds. *The History of Apologetics*. Grand Rapids, MI: Zondervan Academic, 2020.

Frame, John M. *Apologetics: A Justification of Christian Belief*. Edited by Joseph E. Torres. Second edition. Phillipsburg, NJ: Presbyterian and Reformed, 2015.

———. *A History of Western Philosophy and Theology*. 1st ed. Phillipsburg, NJ: Presbyterian and Reformed, 2015.

———. *Perspectives on the Word of God: An Introduction to Christian Ethics*. Phillipsburg, NJ: Presbyterian and Reformed, 1990.

Geffcken, J. "Die Oracula Sibyllina." In *Die griechischen christlichen Schriftsteller*. Edited by Johannes Geffcken, 1–226. Leipzig: Hinrichs, 1902.

Geisler, Norman L. *Inerrancy*. Grand Rapids, MI: Zondervan, 1980.

———. "Irenaeus on Scripture and Tradition." Norman Geisler Blog, 2014. Accessed online: December 18, 2023. https://normangeisler.com/irenaeus-tradition-scripture/

Grant, Robert M. *After the New Testament: Studies in Early Christian Literature and Theology*. Minneapolis, MN: Fortress, 1967.

———. "The Bible of Theophilus of Antioch." *Journal of Biblical Literature* 66, no. 2 (1947) 173–96.

———. "The Decalogue in Early Christianity." *The Harvard Theological Review* 40, no. 1 (1947) 1–17.

———. *Greek Apologists of the Second Century*. 1st ed. Louisville, KY: Westminster John Knox, 1988.

———. *Irenaeus of Lyons*. London; New York: Routledge, 1997.

———. *Jesus after the Gospels: The Christ of the Second Century*. Louisville, KY: Westminster John Knox, 1990.

Bibliography

———. "The Problem of Theophilus." *The Harvard Theological Review*, Vol. 43, No. 3 (Jul., 1950) 179–96

———. "Scripture, Rhetoric and Theology in Theophilus." *Vigiliae Christianae* 13, no. 1 (1959) 33–45.

———. "The Social Setting of Second-Century Christianity." In *Jewish and Christian Self-Definition, Vol. 1: The Shaping of Christianity in the Second and Third Centuries*. 1st American Edition. Edited by E.P. Sanders. Minneapolis, MN: Fortress, 1980. pp. 16–29.

———. "The Textual Tradition of Theophilus of Antioch." *Vigiliae Christianae* 6, no. 3 (1952) 146–59.

———. *Theophilus of Antioch: Ad Autolycum*. Oxford Early Christian Texts. Oxford: Oxford University Press, 1971.

———. "Theophilus of Antioch to Autolycus." *The Harvard Theological Review* 40, no. 4 (1947) 227–56.

Graves, Michael. *The Inspiration and Interpretation of Scripture: What the Early Church Can Teach Us*. Grand Rapids, MI; Cambridge, U.K.: Eerdmans, 2014.

Gregory, Caspar René. "The Reading of Scripture in the Church in the Second Century." *The American Journal of Theology*, Vol. 13, No. 1 (Jan., 1909) 86–91.

Gruen, Erich S. "Jews, Greeks, and Romans in the Third Sibylline Oracle." In *The Construct of Identity in Hellenistic Judaism: Essays on Early Jewish Literature and History*. Berlin; Boston: De Gruyter, 2016. pp. 451–72.

Hahneman, Geoffrey Mark. *The Muratorian Fragment and the Development of the Canon*. Oxford: Oxford University Press, 1992.

Hall, Christopher A. *Learning Theology with the Church Fathers*. Downers Grove, IL: IVP Academic, 2002.

———. *Reading Scripture with the Church Fathers*. Downers Grove, IL: InterVarsity, 1998.

Harnack, Adolf von. *Das Neue Testament um das Jahr 200: Theodor Zahn's Geschichte des neutestamentlichen Kanons (1. Bd., 1 Halfte)*. Freiburg: J. C. B. Mohr, 1889.

———. "Theophilus von Antiochien und das Neue Testament." In *Zeitschriftfur Kirchengeschichte* 11 (1890) 1–21.

Hartog, Paul. *Polycarp and the New Testament: The Occasion, Rhetoric, Theme, and Unity of the Epistle to the Philippians and Its Allusions to the New Testament Literature*. Tübingen: MohrSiebeck, 2002.

Haykin, Michael A. G. *Giving Glory to the Consubstantial Trinity: An Essay on the Quintessence of the Christian Faith*. Greenbrier, AR: Free Grace, 2018.

———. *Rediscovering the Church Fathers: Who They Were and How They Shaped the Church*. Wheaton, IL: Crossway, 2011.

Hays, Richard B. *Echoes of Scripture in the Letters of Paul*. New Haven: Yale University Press, 1989.

Hegesippus. "Fragments from His Five Books of Commentaries on the Acts of the Church." In *Fathers of the Third and Fourth Centuries: The Twelve Patriarchs, Excerpts and Epistles, the Clementina, Apocrypha, Decretals, Memoirs of Edessa and Syriac Documents, Remains of the First Ages*, ed. Alexander Roberts, James Donaldson, and A. Cleveland Coxe, trans. B. P. Pratten, The Ante-Nicene Fathers. Volume 8. Buffalo, NY: Christian Literature Company, 1886.

Hill, Charles E. and Michael J. Kruger, eds. *The Early Text of the New Testament*. Oxford: Oxford University Press, 2014.

Bibliography

Hill, Charles E. "Irenaeus, the Scribes, and the Scriptures Papyrological and Theological Observations from P.Oxy 3.405." In *Irenaeus: Life, Scripture, Legacy,* edited by Sara Parvis and Paul Foster. Minneapolis, MN: Fortresss, 2012.

———. "'The Truth above All Demonstration': Scripture in the Patristic Period to Augustine." In *The Enduring Authority of the Christian Scriptures,* edited by D. A. Carson. Grand Rapids, MI; Cambridge, U.K.: Eerdmans, 2016. pp. 43–88.

Hodge, Charles. *Systematic Theology.* Oak Harbor, WA: Logos Research Systems, 1997.

Holmes, Michael W. "Review of *Polycarp and the New Testament: The Occasion, Rhetoric, Theme, and Unity of the Epistle to the Philippians and Its Allusions to the New Testament Literature* by Paul Hartog." In *Journal of Biblical Literature.* Volume 121, No. 4 (Winter, 2002) 781–3.

Humphrey, Edith M. *Scripture and Tradition: What the Bible Really Says.* Edited by Craig A. Evans and Lee Martin McDonald. Acadia Studies in Bible and Theology. Grand Rapids, MI: Baker Academic, 2013.

Irenaeus of Lyons. *The Writings of Irenæus.* Edited by Alexander Roberts and James Donaldson. Translated by Alexander Roberts and W. H. Rambaut. Vol. 1 & 2. Ante-Nicene Christian Library. Edinburgh: T. & T. Clark; Hamilton & Co.; John Robertson & Co., 1868–1869.

———. *St. Irenaeus of Lyons: Against the Heresies, Book 1.* Edited by Walter J. Burghardt, John J. Dillon, and Thomas Comerford Lawler. Translated by Dominic J. Unger. 55th ed. Vol. I. Ancient Christian Writers. Mahwah, NJ: Newman, 1992.

———. *St. Irenaeus of Lyons: Against the Heresies, Book 2.* Edited by John J. Dillon. Translated by Dominic J. Unger. Vol. 65. Ancient Christian Writers. Mahwah, NJ: Newman, 2012.

———. *The Demonstration of the Apostolic Preaching.* Edited by W. J. Sparrow Simpson and W. K. Lowther Clarke. Translated by J. Armitage Robinson. Translations of Christian Literature. Series IV, Oriental Texts. London; New York: Society for Promoting Christian Knowledge; Macmillan, 1920.

James, Montague Rhode. *The Apocryphal New Testament.* Oxford: Clarendon, 1924.

Jefford, Clayton N. *The Apostolic Fathers and the New Testament.* Peabody, MA: Hendrickson, 2006.

Jerome. *Lives of Illustrious Men.* In *Nicene and Post-Nicene Fathers 2.3: Theodoret, Gennadius, Rufinus: Historical Writings, etc.* Philip Schaff and Henry Wace eds. Buffalo, NY: Christian Literature Company, 1892.

Johnson, Jeffrey. *The Absurdity of Unbelief: A Worldview Apologetic of the Christian Faith.* Conway, AR: Free Grace, 2016.

Josephus, Flavius, and William Whiston. *The Works of Josephus: Complete and Unabridged.* Peabody: Hendrickson, 1987.

Justin Martyr. *St. Justin Martyr: The First and Second Apologies.* Edited by Walter J. Burghardt, John J. Dillon, Dennis D. McManus, and Leslie William Barnard. Translated by Leslie William Barnard. Vol. 56. Ancient Christian Writers. Mahwah, NJ: Paulist, 1997.

Kappler, Werner, ed. *Maccabaeorum Liber II.* Volume IX, 2. Vetus Testamentum Graecum. Auctoritate Academiae Scientiarum Gottingensis editum. Göttingen: Vandenhoeck & Ruprecht, 2008.

Keary, M. B. "Note on ΑΘΗΝΑ ΦΙΛΟΚΟΛΠΟΣ in Theophilus of Antioch." *Revue des Études Grecques,* Vol. 84, No. 399/400 (Jan.–June, 1971) 94–100.

Kelly, J. N. D. *Early Christian Doctrines.* Fifth, Revised. London: Bloomsbury, 1977.

Bibliography

King, David T. and William Webster. *Holy Scripture: The Ground and Pillar of Our Faith.* 3 vols. Battle Ground, WA: Christian Resources, 2001.

Kistler, Don, ed. *Sola Scriptura: The Protestant Position on the Bible.* Lake Mary, FL: Reformation Trust, 2009.

Köstenberger, Andreas J., and Michael J. Kruger. *The Heresy of Orthodoxy: How Contemporary Culture's Fascination with Diversity Has Reshaped Our Understanding of Early Christianity.* Wheaton, IL: Crossway, 2010.

Kraft, Robert A. "Review of *Theophilus of Antioch, Ad Autolycum* by Robert M. Grant." *Journal of Biblical Literature*, Vol. 91, No. 1 (Mar., 1972) 126–28.

Kruger, Michael J. "The Authenticity of 2 Peter." *Journal of Evangelical Theological Society* 42.4 (December 1999) 643–78.

———. *Canon Revisited: Establishing the Origins and Authority of the New Testament Books.* Wheaton, IL: Crossway, 2012.

———. *Christianity at the Crossroads: How the Second Century Shaped the Future of the Church.* Downers Grove, IL: InterVarsity, 2018.

———. "The Definition of the Term 'Canon': Exclusive or Multi-Dimensional?" *Tyndale Bulletin* 63, no. 1 (2012) 1–20.

———. *The Question of Canon: Challenging the Status Quo in the New Testament Debate.* Downers Grove, IL: InterVarsity, 2013.

Lashier, Jackson Jay, "The Trinitarian Theology of Irenaeus of Lyons." PhD Dissertation. Marquette University, 2011. Accessed online on December 20, 2023. http://epublications.marquette.edu/dissertations_mu/109

Law, Timothy Michael. *When God Spoke Greek: The Septuagint and the Making of the Christian Bible.* Oxford: Oxford University Press, 2013.

Lawson, John. *The Biblical Theology of Saint Irenaeus.* Eugene, OR: Wipf and Stock, 2006.

Letham, Robert. "Early Trinitarianism." In *The Holy Trinity: In Scripture, History, Theology, and Worship.* Kindle edition. Phillipsburg, NJ: Presbyterian and Reformed, 2004. pp. 85–104.

Lightfoot, J. L. *The Sibylline Oracles.* Oxford: Oxford University Press, 2007.

Litfin, Bryan M. "Tertullian on the Trinity." *Perichoresis*, vol. 17.1 (2019) 81–98.

Loofs, Friedrich. *Theophilus von Antiochen Adversus Marcionem und die Anderen Theologischen Quellen bei Irenaeus.* Texte und Untersuchungen zur Geschichte der altchristlichen Literatur, no. 46.2. Leipzig: J. C. Hinrichs, 1930.

Marcovich, Miroslav. "Theophilus of Antioch: Fifty-five Emendations." *Illinois Classical Studies*, Vol. 4 (1979) 76–93.

Malina, Bruce J. "Jewish Christianity or Christian Judaism: Toward a Hypothetical Definition." *Journal for the Study of Judaism in the Persian, Hellenistic, and Roman Period* 7, no. 1 (1976) 46–57.

Martin, José Pablo. "Filón Hebreo y Teofilo Cristiano: La Continuidad de una Teología Natural." *Salmanticensis* 152 (1986) 301–17.

———. "La Presencia de Filón en el Hexameron de Teófilo de Antioquía." *Salmanticensis* (1986) Vol 33, No. 2: 147–77.

Mathison, Keith A. *The Shape of Sola Scriptura.* Moscow, IN: Canon, 2001.

McDonald, Lee Martin and James A. Sanders, eds. *The Canon Debate.* Peabody, MA: Hendrickson, 2002.

McVey, Kathleen E. "The Use of Stoic Cosmogony in Theophilus of Antioch's *Hexaemeron*." In *Biblical Hermeneutics in Historical Perspective: Studies in Honor of Karlfried*

Bibliography

Froehlich on His Sixtieth Birthday. Edited by Mark S. Burrows and Paul Rorem, 32–58. Grand Rapids, MI: Eerdmans, 1991.

Metzger, Bruce M. *The Canon of the New Testament: Its Origin, Development, and Significance*. Oxford: Oxford University Press, 1997.

———. "Literary Forgeries and Canonical Pseudepigrapha." *Journal of Biblical Literature*, Vol. 91, No. 1 (March, 1972) 3–24.

———, and Bart D. Ehrman. *The Text of the New Testament: Its Transmission, Corruption, and Restoration*. 4th ed. Oxford: Oxford University Press, 2005.

Minns, Denis. *Irenaeus: An Introduction*. London; New York: T&T Clark, 2010.

Moo, Douglas J. *The Letters to the Colossians and to Philemon*. The Pillar New Testament Commentary. Grand Rapids, MI: Eerdmans, 2008.

Morales Escobar, Daniel. "Los Tres Libros a Autólico de Teófilo de Antiouqía y la Actitud Política de los Crisitanos en el Siglo II." Universidad de Salamanca. *Studia Historica: Historia Antigua*. Volume 2. (2009) 193–8.

Needham, Nick. *2,000 Years of Christ's Power: The Age of the Early Church Fathers*. Volume 1. Scotland, UK: Christian Focus, 2016.

O'Keefe, John J. and R. R. Reno. *Sanctified Vision: An Introduction to Early Christian Interpretation of the Bible*. Baltimore, MD: Johns Hopkins University Press, 2005.

Orr, James. *The History and Literature of the Early Church*. London: Hodder and Stoughton, 1913.

Osborne, Eric. *The Emergence of Christian Theology*. Cambridge: Cambridge University Press, 1993.

———. *Irenaeus of Lyons*. Cambridge; New York: Cambridge University Press, 2004.

Otto, Karl. "Gebrauch neutestamentlicher Schriften bei Theophilus von Antiochien." In *Zeitschrift fur historische Theologie* 29 (1859) 617–22.

Oxford Society of Historical Theology. *The New Testament in the Apostolic Fathers*. Bellingham, WA: Logos Research Systems, 2009.

Paget, James Carleton and Judith Lieu. *Christianity in the Second Century: Themes and Developments*. Cambridge: Cambridge University Press, 2017.

Parke, H.W. "The Sibyl in Christian Literature." In *Sibyls and Sibylline Prophecy in Classical Antiquity*, 152–73. New York: Routledge, 2014.

Parsons, Stuart. *Ancient Apologetic Exegesis: Introducing and Recovering Theophilus's World*. Eugene, OR: Pickwick, 2015.

———. and D. Jeffrey Bingham. "'By One and the Same Spirit': Inspired Texts in Theophilus of Antioch's 'Ad Autolycum.'" PhD Dissertation. Dallas Theological Seminary. Ann Arbor, MI: ProQuest Dissertations Publishing, 2005.

———. "Trading Places: Faithful Job and Doubtful Autolycus in Theophilus's Apology." In *Studia Patristica XCIII: Papers presented at the Seventeenth International Conference on Patristic Studies held in Oxford 2015. Volume 19: The First Two Centuries; Apocrypha and Gnostica*, edited by Markus Vinznet, 191–7. Leuven: Peeters, 2017.

———. "Very Early Trinitarian Expressions." *Tyndale Bulletin* 65, no. 1 (2014) 141–52.

Parvis, Sara and Paul Foster, eds. *Irenaeus: Life, Scripture, Legacy*. Minneapolis, MN: Fortress, 2012.

Pascal, Bennett. "Review of *Theophilus of Antioch, Ad Autolycum* by Robert M. Grant." *The Classical World*, Vol. 65, No. 3 (Nov. 1971) 94–5.

Poirier, John C. "Stuart Parsons: *Ancient Apologetic Exegesis*." *The Pneuma Review* (October 12, 2017). Accessed Online December 18, 2023. http://pneumareview.com/stuart-parsons-ancient-apologetic-exegesis/

Bibliography

Quasten, Johannes, and Joseph C. Plumpe, eds. *The Didache, The Epistle of Barnabas, The Epistles and the Martyrdom of St. Polycarp, The Fragments of Papias and The Epistle to Diognetus.* Translated by James A. Kleist. 6th ed. Ancient Christian Writers. New York: Newman, 1948.

Reuss, Eduard Wilhelm Eugen. *History of the Sacred Scriptures of the New Testament.* Translated by Edward L. Houghton. Vol. I & II. Boston, MD: Houghton, Mifflin and Company, 1884.

Roberts, Alexander, James Donaldson, and A. Cleveland Coxe, eds. *The Apostolic Fathers with Justin Martyr and Irenaeus.* Volume 1. The Ante-Nicene Fathers. Buffalo, NY: Christian Literature Company, 1885.

———. *Fathers of the Second Century: Hermas, Tatian, Athenagoras, Theophilus, and Clement of Alexandria (Entire).* Volume 2. The Ante-Nicene Fathers. Buffalo, NY: Christian Literature Company, 1885.

———. *Fathers of the Third and Fourth Centuries: The Twelve Patriarchs, Excerpts and Epistles, the Clementina, Apocrypha, Decretals, Memoirs of Edessa and Syriac Documents, Remains of the First Ages.* Volume 8. The Ante-Nicene Fathers. Buffalo, NY: Christian Literature Company, 1886.

Rogers, Rick. "Theophilus of Antioch." *The Expository Times.* Volume 120, No. 5 (2009) 214–24.

———. *Theophilus of Antioch: The Life and Thought of a Second-Century Bishop.* Boston, MD: Lexington, 2000.

Sanday, William. "A Commentary on the Gospels Attributed to Theophilus of Antioch." In *Studia Biblica et Ecclesiastica,* 89–101. Oxford: Clarendon, 1885.

Sanders, E.P., ed. *Jewish and Christian Self-Definition, Vol. 1: The Shaping of Christianity in the Second and Third Centuries.* 1st American Edition. Minneapolis, MN: Fortress, 1980.

Schaff, Philip, and David Schley Schaff. *History of the Christian Church.* 8 vols. New York: Charles Scribner's Sons, 1910.

Schoedel, William R. "Theophilus of Antioch: Jewish Christian?" *Illinois Classical Studies* 18 (1993) 279–97.

Schröter, Jens. *From Jesus to the New Testament: Early Christian Theology and the Origin of the New Testament Canon.* Edited by Wayne Coppins and Simon Gathercole. Translated by Wayne Coppins. Baylor-Mohr Siebeck Studies in Early Christianity. Waco, TX: Baylor University Press; Mohr Siebeck, 2013.

Shedd, William G. T. *A History of Christian Doctrine.* Volume 1. Eugene, OR: Wipf and Stock, 1999.

Simonetti, Manlio. "La Sacra Scrittura in Teofilo D'Antiochia." In *Epektasis: Melanges patristiques offerts au Cardinal Jean Danielou,* ed. Jacques Fontaine and Charles Kannengiesser, 197–207. Paris: Editions Beauchesne, 1972.

Skarsaune, Oskar. "Heresy and the Pastoral Epistles." *Themelios* 20, no. 1 (1994) 9–13.

Stanglin, Keith D. *The Letter and Spirit of Biblical Interpretation: From the Early Church to Modern Practice.* Grand Rapids, MI: Baker Academic, 2018.

Steenberg, Matthew C. "To Test or Preserve? The Prohibition of Gen. 2:16–17 in the Thought of Two Second-Century Exegetes." *Gregorianum* Vol. 86, No. 4 (2005) 723–41.

Steinmetz, David C. "The Superiority of Pre-critical Exegesis." In *Taking the Long View: Christian Theology in Historical Perspective,* 3–14. Oxford: Oxford University Press, 2011.

Bibliography

Stevenson, James. *A New Eusebius: Documents Illustrating the History of the Church to AD 337*. London: SPCK, 1987.

Stonehouse, N.B. and Paul Woolley, eds. *The Infallible Word: A Symposium by the Members of the Faculty of Westminster Theological Seminary*. 2nd ed. Phillipsburg, NJ: Presbyterian and Reformed, 2002.

Sundberg, Albert C. Jr. "The Bible Canon and the Christian Doctrine of Inspiration." *Interpretation*. Sage, 1975.

———. "Canon Muratori: A Fourth-Century List." *Harvard Theological Review* 66 (1973) 1–41.

———. "The Making of the New Testament Canon." In *The Interpreter's One-Volume Commentary on the Bible*. Edited by Charles M. Laymon, 1216–24. Nashville: Abingdon, 1971.

———. "The Old Testament of the Early Church (A Study in Canon)." *The Harvard Theological Review* 51, no. 4 (1958) 205–26.

Svebakken, Hans. "Theophilus of Antioch." In *The Dictionary of Historical Theology*. Edited by Trevor Hart, 542–43. Grand Rapids, MI: Eerdmans, 2000.

Taylor, Joan. "The Phenomenon of Early Jewish-Christianity: Reality or Scholarly Invention?" *Vigiliae Christianae* 44 (1990) 313–34.

Tyson, Joseph B. *The New Testament and Early Christianity*. New York: MacMillan, 1984.

Van Til, Cornelius. *The Defense of the Faith*. 1st ed. Philadelphia, PA: Presbyterian and Reformed, 1955.

Vermande, Jean-Marie. "Théophile d'Antioche contre Celse; A Autolycos III." *REAug* 17 (1971) 102–23.

Warfield, Benjamin B. "Authority and Inspiration of Scripture." In *Selected Shorter Writings*, volume 2. Edited by John E. Meeter. Phillipsburg, NJ: Presbyterian and Reformed, 2001.

———. *The Canon of the New Testament: How and When Formed*. Philadelphia, PA: American Sunday-School Union, 1892.

———. *The Works of Benjamin B. Warfield: Revelation and Inspiration*. Vol. 1. Bellingham, WA: Logos Bible Software, 2008.

Weinrich, William C. "*Theophilus of Antioch: Life and Thought of a Second-Century Bishop* (review)" *Journal of Early Christian Studies*. Volume 9, No. 4 (Winter, 2001) 601–3.

Whittaker, Molly. "Review of *Theophilus of Antioch: Ad Autolycum* (Oxford Early Christian Texts) by Robert M. Grant." *The Journal of Theological Studies*. New Series, Vol. 23, No. 1 (April, 2972) 235–6.

Wilken, Robert Louis. *The Spirit of Early Christian Thought: Seeking the Face of God*. Kindle Edition. New Haven: Yale University Press, 2003.

Williams, D. H. *Evangelicals and Tradition: The Formative Influence of the Early Church*. Evangelical Ressourcement. Grand Rapids, MI: Baker Academic, 2005.

———. *Retrieving the Tradition & Renewing Evangelicalism: A Primer for Suspicious Protestants*. Grand Rapids, MI: Eerdmans, 1999.

———. ed. *Tradition, Scripture, and Interpretation: A Sourcebook of the Ancient Church*. Evangelical Ressourcement. Grand Rapids, MI: Baker Academic, 2006.

Young, Frances M. "The Rhetorical Schools and Their Influence on Patristic Exegesis." In *The Making of Orthodoxy: Essays in Honour of Henry Chadwick*. Edited by Rowan Williams, 182–99. Cambridge: Cambridge University Press, 1989.

———. "Greek Apologists of the Second Century." In *Apologetics in the Roman Empire: Pagans, Jews, and Christians*. Edited by Mark J. Edwards, Martin Goodman, Simon Price, Chris Rowland, 81–104. Oxford: Oxford University Press, 1999.

www.ingramcontent.com/pod-product-compliance
Lightning Source LLC
Chambersburg PA
CBHW060820190426
43197CB00038B/2165